REVIVE

Bringing Health, Vitality, and Growth
Back into Your Church

THE REV CANON MARK ELDREDGE

American Anglican
Press

Published by the American Anglican Council.

Designed and edited by F.G. Capitanio and Bev Mueffelmann.

Cover Photo by Photo by Tangerine Newt on Unsplash

ISBN: 979-8-9853941-0-8

This book is dedicated to:

Christ Church Midland, Texas
who gave me the freedom to first put these church health principles
into practice; and to Christ Church Jacksonville who together for 14
years revived and saw many lives changed for good.

TABLE OF CONTENTS

FOREWORD

I have had the privilege of knowing the Rev. Canon Mark Eldredge for a good number of years. Throughout my time with the Anglican Church in North America, he and his beard have graced Provincial Councils, assemblies, and conferences, and while the length of his beard may change, one thing has never changed about him: his passion for the Gospel and for church revitalization. I've always known him as a man comfortable with telling people about Jesus. The call for personal renewal, as this book explains, is the place where revitalization begins; the Gospel and the Church can't be separated. And wherever we push forward in the quest for growth, if Jesus is not the first and main reason for the message, it's a fruitless endeavor. It's growth for the sake of growth, rather than for the sake of a healthier community in which the individual can find their own healing and restoration through Jesus Christ. That's the heart of the revived church.

Canon Mark has always been, to those of us who

know him, a man of action. I'm sure this book is one of those actions taken not just to give people something new to fill their bookshelves, another "How-to", but to give leaders a plan of action for themselves. It's a book that lays out steps for moving towards health born out of Canon Mark's personal experience. His own revitalization began with an encounter with Jesus and continued with an encounter with Jesus' people as a parish priest. It continues today with his work in the American Anglican Council, a ministry that the ACNA holds dear as we partner together for the sake of the Gospel in North America.

As North America continues embracing the Western humanist mindset, the Gospel gets harder to see through all the chaos. The complexities and confusions of our society continue to grow. Technology has expanded our connectivity, opening windows into private lives that, come to think of it, should perhaps never have been opened. Electronics become the medium through which we hear the clamoring of politics and the so-called culture wars, and the latest tweet and soundbite become fodder for an ongoing fire of activism, discontent, and perplexity. The current "choose your side" mentality is not just the product of American politics or culture wars. Humans have been dividing themselves into factions with little hope of resolve since Adam pointed his guilty finger at Eve and said, "The woman made me do it." With that moment in time, the blame game came in, along with sin and darkness, and today, as our culture embraces that darkness, some individuals within it are struggling to encounter the light. Those are the ones we are called to save and then serve. But the noise of so many voices make it harder for us to say what we need to say for the sake of those looking for answers in the craziness. How do we, as church leaders, engage our churches and our neighborhoods in this new age of division, doubt, and darkness? How do we get through the noise and get back to the essentials of the Gospel, especially for those hungry for the light? How do we build stronger, healthier communities that can bring healing to those same people, no matter what they've been through?

In my own experience, I've seen the ACNA provide light to so many as her parishioners pulled away from a church that already entered and embraced the culture behind closed doors, in the dark. Those who led people away from the blindness began building a mansion with many rooms and many windows. Churches needed to be planted and some needed to be revitalized. We had success and, through faithful workers in the field, we grew. Canon Mark was a part of that, and though the last decade has been one of growth, the struggle continues. We still need revitalization. The Church is only as strong as its next generation.

Canon Mark has a passion for church leaders and communities struggling for health. Revive shows that. But it's not just passion and excitement talking; it's also practical step-by-step help for leaders to utilize as they move towards real and lasting change. Revive is an attempt to coax some of us out of our neatly classified ways of thinking and our old ways of being and into a new paradigm of health and spiritual prosperity. Here, we can ask questions about what to do, find ways to talk with others experiencing the same struggles, and boldly move forward with the communities entrusted to our care without fear and with solid guidance. Church is, for Canon Mark, not just a duty for leaders to fulfill but a place of opportunity, where exploration can occur freely, where creative minds are freed to find new ways of engaging the communities they find themselves in, and where God brings new life and new light to those around us. I am thankful to him for his willingness to speak out in the cultural chaos around us, to add his voice to the many voices across our great province who preach and teach our churches to hope for the Kingdom to Come wherever God placed them. It is my hope that those who pick up this book will have their own journey, wherever they find themselves, and end up finding that the monumental task of church revitalization should be a promising adventure and a not-so-scary thing to hope for after all.

- The Rt. Rev. Alan Hawkins
  Chief Operating Officer, Anglican Church in North America

INTRODUCTION

Any local church can be revived by bringing renewal, church health, and growth. This book is written for both clergy and laity in existing churches experiencing a season of plateau or decline. Although primarily written with Anglican churches in mind, everything in this book is applicable to any Christian church. So, if you picked up this book, regardless of your denomination, I trust it was a prompt from the Lord, and I encourage you to read on!

At the end of each of the five sections, as well as after several chapters, there are questions to use either individually or in a group to help apply the concepts from that section in your church. Although it can be read straight through in a sitting or two, this book was designed with the idea that you could read one chapter a day over about six weeks to let the concepts in the 40 chapters really sink in. This design makes it an ideal read during church seasons like Epiphany, Lent, and Easter with a small group or even a vestry/parish council discussing it and applying it in the church.

Revive is also the title of the American Anglican Council (AAC) church revitalization seminar and coaching process. Although there are certainly overlaps in the concepts between book and seminar, both are helpful in their own unique way. In both this book and the seminar/coaching process, the word "REVIVE" is an acrostic that stands for REnewal, Vision & Values, Insistence on church health, Vital strategies, and Enacting the vision. That acrostic is the outline for the five sections in this book. Each chapter is designed to give you a vision for a preferred future of health and growth, motivation to put that vision into action, and the means to accomplish it.

Each chapter is an adaptation of a series of individual articles I wrote for the American Anglican Council's weekly newsletter. The response to those articles was so positive that, rather than let them linger, it seemed good to put them into book form. If you find the ideas in this book to be helpful to you and your church, you can find other church revitalization resources at www.churchrevive.org and prayerfully consider having us come and provide the complete Revive seminar and coaching process in your congregation. You may also visit www.americananglican.org to find out more information on the American Anglican Council and what's happening in the Anglican Church around the world.

SECTION ONE:

THE CORNERSTONE OF REVITALIZATION

And he said to him, "You shall love the Lord your God with all your heart and with all your soul and with all your mind. This is the great and first commandment. And a second is like it: You shall love your neighbor as yourself. On these two commandments depend all the Law and the Prophets."

Matthew 22:37-40

CHAPTER 1:
FIVE RENEWALS FOR REVITALIZATION

One of the most helpful bits of information about church revitalization that I've learned is "when God wants to revitalize a church, he takes them through five types of renewal. These never happen out of order." That is a bold statement I've found to be true. Renewal is the cornerstone of church revitalization. The five types of renewal are Personal, Relational, Missional, Structural, and Cultural.

When a church is in the life cycle stage of recline (having plateaued) or decline and decides to work on revitalization, most of the time the first instinct is to jump right to the fourth renewal: structural. This makes sense because structures deal with possible solutions that are the most easily visible.

I live in Florida, and as I write this it is May and already 98 degrees. My air conditioner is straining to keep the house cool. We had an expert come assess the house to see what we could do to help. Our first guess given the house's age was to upgrade the windows because we can see they are old, and we feel the heat coming in through them. The expert we hired, however, said that while it's not bad to address upgrading the windows, it isn't the best or most cost-effective solution. By far the better strategy would be to add insulation to the attic which costs less and would have a greater impact on keeping the house cooler. Since people don't see the attic, this better solution is often overlooked, and people spend a ton of money on windows with very few results.

This is often how it works with church revitalization. The thought is that if we can just reorganize the organization, make some tweaks here and there to ministries, or add just the right program then things will turn around. Those are not bad things, however, doing them first without engaging in the first three renewals usually doesn't result in growth. A lot of time and energy are spent with few results, and then people get mad and think revitalization doesn't work.

When the prophet Samuel looked first to David's older brother Eliab and assumed, he must be the one to anoint, "The Lord said to Samuel, 'Do not consider his appearance or his height, for I have rejected him. The Lord does not look at the things people look at. People look at the outward appearance, but the Lord looks at the heart.'" (1 Samuel 16:7) If you want to see your church grow, avoid looking first at the outward structural issues and instead look at the heart, just as God does with us. The way to look at the heart of a matter is by addressing the first three renewals: Personal, Relational, and Missional, leaving Structural for later. We can simply summarize them with this question: Is your church truly committed to obeying the Great Commandment and the Great Commission? The following two scriptures capture the heart of these three renewals:

The Great Commandment: 'Love the Lord your God with all your heart and with all your soul and with all your mind.' This is the first and greatest commandment. And the second is like it: 'Love your neighbor as yourself.' (Matthew 22:37-39)

The Great Commission: Then Jesus came to them and said, "All authority in heaven and on earth has been given to me. Therefore, go and make disciples of all nations, baptizing them in the name of the Father and of the Son and of the Holy Spirit, and teaching them to obey everything I have commanded you. And surely, I am with you always, to the very end of the age." (Matthew 28:18-20)

When thinking about personal renewal, do you and others in your church truly love the Lord with everything you have? Is the goal of abiding in his love (John 15) and doing life with him your absolute priority? Is there a deep passion for real relationship with Jesus through the Holy Spirit running throughout your congregation? This kind of personal love for Jesus will do more for church growth than any amount of structural changes, important as they might be!

When thinking about relational renewal, do you and others in your church truly love one another? Are you quick to forgive one another? Is there genuine care for each other when you are together that a visitor would sense and want to be a part your community? Unchurched visitors can sort of "smell it" if love is not there, and they may instinctively not want anything to do with you!

When thinking about missional renewal, do you and others in your church truly love lost outsiders? Do you see those around you who are unchurched with sincere compassion rather than judgment? Do you see that they are either visibly or invisibly broken due to the world, the flesh, or the devil? And, in love, do want them to know the way, the truth, and the life - Jesus? Does your love for lost sinners compel you to go to them in order to make them disciples of Jesus, too?

Even though these kinds of renewal are not as easily seen as structural needs, being renewed with genuine love for the Lord, for one another, and for the lost will do more for your church in the long run.

CHAPTER 2:
PERSONAL RENEWAL

When diving more deeply into personal renewal, how can you experience it both individually and as a congregation? These five principles can help foster that renewal, which comes only by the Holy Spirit.

Being Born Again

Jesus spoke to Nicodemus about being born again when he taught that, "No one can enter the Kingdom of God without being born of water and the Spirit. Humans can reproduce only human life, but the Holy Spirit gives birth to spiritual life. So, don't be surprised when I say, 'You must be born again.'" (John 3:5-7 NLT) You can never be spiritually renewed if you've never been made new in the first place. Believing in Jesus' death and resurrection, asking for the forgiveness of your sins, and receiving the Holy Spirit into your life is foundational to transformation. If you're not sure if you have been born again, and you're not sure exactly how to become born again, I recommend you talk to your priest/pastor. The one thing you can do now to start that conversation is to pray the following prayer, believing it in your heart:

"Lord, I admit that I have turned from your ways and done things that are wrong. Thank you, Jesus, that you came, died, and rose again to take away all my sin. Please forgive me. I receive your forgiveness now and declare that I want to live for you for the rest of my life. Come and fill my life with your Holy Spirit. Help me now to depend completely on you. Amen."

Being Baptized in the Holy Spirit

Jesus commanded his disciples: "Do not leave Jerusalem until the Father sends you the gift he promised, as I told you before. John baptized with water, but in just a few days you will be baptized with the Holy Spirit." (Acts 1:4-5 NLT) This was after the resurrection and after the disciples were born again. They had already received the Holy Spirit in the upper room when Jesus first appeared to them. It says in John 20:21-22, "Again [Jesus] said, 'Peace be with you. As the Father has sent me, so I am sending you.' Then he breathed on them and said, 'Receive the Holy Spirit.'" (NLT) Despite their reception of the Spirit, Jesus commanded the disciples to wait for the baptism with the Holy Spirit still to come.

If the disciples needed this baptism to have the power to spread the Kingdom of God, then why should we think we can grow the church without having this baptism for ourselves? If you desire more of the Spirit's power or if you have never received it, here's a prayer you can sincerely pray in order to receive this power to serve: "Heavenly Father, I thank You that Jesus saved me, and I pray that the Holy Spirit might come upon me now. Lord, Jesus Christ, baptize me now in the Holy Spirit, for I am willing to receive all that He has for me right now by faith in Your Word. May the anointing, the glory, and the power of God come upon me and into my life. May I be empowered for service from this day forward. Thank You, Lord Jesus, for Your Holy Spirit. Amen."

Being Bold in Your Witness

Jesus said, "But you will receive power when the Holy Spirit comes upon you. And you will be my witnesses, telling people about me everywhere—in Jerusalem, throughout Judea, in Samaria, and to the ends of the earth." (Acts 1:8 NLT) Enjoying a personal relationship with Jesus through the Holy Spirit and experiencing the transformation that he brings is wonderful. This transformation isn't, however, only about you. We must experience new life in order to share new life. The mission is by both demonstration and proclamation in order to bear witness to the Kingdom of God on earth as it is in heaven. Make sure, as you experience personal renewal, that you let it overflow out of you and into the world around you. As individuals in the Church community encounter Jesus, they can begin to process that transformation with one another and ultimately go out together into the world. But how do you foster this kind of personal and yet communal renewal?

Being Preachers and Teachers of a Personal Relationship with Jesus

There is a leadership principle that says that you get more of what you focus on. If you focus the preaching and teaching on giving, giving will increase. If you focus on serving, you'll see more people serving, and so on. If your congregation needs more personal renewal, take a season to focus on it in sermons, classes, small groups, and prayer. Make sure to give "How To" directions not just "Ought To" instructions. Teach those in your community to practice the personal spiritual disciplines of worship, prayer, fasting, and giving. It may be "basic" stuff, but if you don't have a strong foundation, the church may never experience revitalization.

Being Providers of Personal Renewal

Prayerfully find good church-wide programs that will help renew everyone's personal relationship with Jesus. Many churches utilize the Alpha program or Christianity Explored. My own church used several 40-Day Spiritual Growth Campaigns like the 40 Days of Purpose and 40 Days of Community campaigns by Pastor Rick Warren.

Knowing how important personal renewal is to a church's revitalization process, the American Anglican Council (AAC) offers spiritual renewal weekends called Renew, where we bring a small team to your church for a weekend of teaching, testimonies, and most importantly, prayer ministry for renewal in the Holy Spirit. This could be a great jump start to your revitalization efforts.

God knows your congregation better than anyone. Ask Him to guide you towards just the right program(s) that will fit your church's renewal needs. He wants you and your church to be passionate for Jesus and filled with the power of the Spirit, so he will lead you to just the right tools!

CHAPTER 3:
RELATIONAL RENEWAL

Relational Renewal comes right from Jesus' Great Commandment, "Love the Lord your God with all your heart and with all your soul and with all your mind. This is the first and greatest commandment. And the second is like it: Love your neighbor as yourself." (Matthew 22:37-39 NIV) Loving others, especially our brothers and sisters in Christ, is high on the priority list for living in God's Kingdom. Just look at this small sample from God's Word:

"So now I am giving you a new commandment: Love each other. Just as I have loved you, you should love each other. Your love for one another will prove to the world that you are my disciples." (John 13:34-35 NLT)

"Owe nothing to anyone—except for your obligation to love one another. If you love your neighbor, you will fulfill the requirements of God's law." (Romans 13:8 NLT)

"And may the Lord make your love for one another and for all people grow and overflow, just as our love for you overflows." (1 Thessalonians 3:12 NLT)

"And this is his commandment: We must believe in the name of his Son, Jesus Christ, and love one another, just as he commanded us." (1 John 3:23 NLT)

"Dear friends, let us continue to love one another, for love comes from God. Anyone who loves is a child of God and knows God." (1 John 4:7 NLT)

"Love means doing what God has commanded us, and he has commanded us to love one another, just as you heard from the beginning." (2 John 1:6 NLT)

If your church is not obedient to this commandment of Jesus, and there is not a genuine love for one another amongst you, then why would he bless your church with growth? Why would non-believers even want to come? If personal renewal begins to take place, however, and its overflow reaches one another, then relational renewal will follow and lead to revitalization.

Entire books could be written on this topic alone, but to help you get some footing in relational renewal, here are just two obstacles to loving one another we can personally avoid and two ways to facilitate genuine love for one another.

Obstacle 1: Defending Biblical Truth vs. Loving Others

For many years while rightly defending Biblical truth, I became defensive against all the talk about love because the term was often used to make excuses for sin. I feared that by embracing love too much, I would begin to slip into liberalism, down the slippery slope to becoming someone who justifies wrong-living and a lack of truth! Of course, I always knew that love was in the Bible. I knew that God is love! But deep down, I was more comfortable focusing on other theological matters, especially during the culture wars I found myself in. Once I became aware of this internal conflict, I was able to process it a bit more and realized that by not fully embracing Jesus' command to love, I wasn't practicing the Biblical truth I so wanted to defend! Defending Biblical truth and truly loving others are not in conflict. We can do both! Jesus did.

A church full of people focused on Biblical truth but not on loving one another won't have the kind of relational renewal needed to bring about revitalization. Paul wrote in 1 Corinthians 13:2, "If I had the gift of prophecy, and if I understood all of God's secret plans and possessed all knowledge, and if I had such faith that I could move mountains, but didn't love others, I would be nothing." So, it's best to be on your guard against these kinds of fears that can prevent you from fully embracing Jesus' command to love others no matter who they are.

Obstacle 2: Making Rituals More Important Than Relationships

Anglicans love liturgy and ritual. It's part of our

heritage. If being Anglican becomes more about the rituals than it does about love, however, then we've missed something important. If the Apostle Paul were writing 1 Corinthians 13 to Anglicans (or any other liturgical Christian tradition), he might have written something like, "If I could have the perfect liturgy, with the perfect choir, and everything done exactly right, but didn't love others, I would only be a noisy gong or a clanging cymbal."

To have a revitalized, healthy, growing Anglican church, the main thing must remain the main thing, and the main thing is Jesus Christ and His Great Commandment to love God and love your neighbor. So, we must be on our guard against letting our traditions, which are created to point us to Christ, become more important than Christ Himself and the people He is calling us to love.

Approach to Love 1: Preaching and Teaching on Loving One Another

As written in the previous chapter, there is a leadership principle that says you get more of what you focus on. If you focus preaching and teaching on giving, giving will increase. If you focus on serving, you'll see more people serve, and so on. If your congregation needs more relational renewal, take time to focus on it through your sermons, small groups, classes, and prayer, remembering to give "How To" directions rather than just "Ought To" instructions. Teach on what it means to live in the Kingdom of God on earth now. I recommend referring to Dallas Willard's materials on this subject. His teaching on the Sermon on the Mount is particularly helpful on how to practice loving one another and can currently be found on YouTube.

Approach to Love 2: Providing "Laboratories" of Love

The local church, like marriage, is an institution that God gave to teach us to love and be loved. Like in marriage, we will find it is sometimes difficult in the church to love and be loveable. As believers, we are all broken though in the process of being made whole in Christ. God has provided the Church as a safe place, a hospital for sinners, where we can heal and grow in Christ over time. A significant part of that healing and growth is learning to love, especially when it's hard. The local church becomes our laboratory to experiment with showing love to one another.

Unless your congregation has less than a dozen members, this laboratory needs small study groups where individuals can find more authentic relationships. It is easy to fake being loving in a large worship setting on Sunday mornings where you are mostly listening anyway. It is much harder to fake it in small groups or ministry teams where lives interact and feelings get hurt, people disappoint, annoying personalities are exposed (yours and others'!), and you must put love into practice.

Providing small groups is an intentional process of church leadership, but it's worth it for facilitating relational renewal. I often get asked the question of how you get people into small groups. One answer is just one word:

fast. A bunch of small groups can start at the same time. One of the best ways I've seen this happen is by using church-wide spiritual growth campaigns that bring the whole church into alignment on one theme for usually about six weeks. We did a campaign on relational renewal called 40 Days of Community designed to "deepen the community in your church and reach out to the community around your church." Groups that formed during that campaign are still meeting today over a decade later. You better believe those folks have seriously learned to love one another.

CHAPTER 4:
MISSIONAL RENEWAL

Most practicing Christians have heard of the Great Commission. In Matthew 28:18-20, it says, "And Jesus came and said to them, 'All authority in heaven and on earth has been given to me. Go therefore and make disciples of all nations, baptizing them in the name of the Father and of the Son and of the Holy Spirit, teaching them to observe all that I have commanded you. And behold, I am with you always, to the end of the age.'" (ESV)

You may have read this before, but did you know there are five Great Commissions? In all four Gospels and in the Book of Acts, Jesus gives some variation of this sending of the disciples out on mission. You can look up the other four in Mark 16:15, Luke 24:46-49, John 20:21, and Acts 1:8. This commissioning is repeated to emphasize that as disciples of Jesus, we are a sent people.

To be clear, this sending out on mission is to be done on the foundations of personal and relational renewal. In Acts 1:4-5 Jesus said, "Do not leave Jerusalem, but wait for the gift my Father promised, which you have heard me speak about. For John baptized with water, but in a few days, you will be baptized with the Holy Spirit." (NIV) In other words, don't try to do the mission without the presence and power of the Holy Spirit who brings about personal renewal. Then just prior to his death and resurrection, Jesus couldn't have been clearer about the need for relational renewal when he said, "A new command I give you: Love one another. As I have loved you, so you must love one another. By this everyone will know that you are my disciples, if you love one another" (John 13:34-35 NIV).

With a real love for God and a real love for one another, we are then commanded to "Go therefore" out into the world to really love non-believers and do whatever it takes to reach them and bring them into God's Kingdom.

The question is how we do that presently and moving forward? It seems to me that Jesus' words in the Great Commission in John 20:21 some two thousand years ago, are still very applicable to us today. "Peace be with you!" he said. "As the Father has sent me, I am sending you." (NIV) As he was sent, we are sent. As he did, so we should do. As he, so we…There are four ways to be on mission as Jesus was.

Leave Our Comfort Zones

"In the beginning was the Word, and the Word was with God, and the Word was God. He was in the beginning with God…And the Word became flesh and dwelt among us" (John 1:1-2,14a ESV). To fulfill the Father's mission to save us, Jesus left heaven and came into our dark world. Can you imagine what it was like for Jesus to leave His glory? It was certainly a loss of divine comforts, and as he was sent, so are we. Though none of us will lose our comforts to the extent that Jesus did, we must be willing to leave our comfort zones to whatever degree may be needed.

One of those comfort zones might be the four walls of the church. Jesus didn't stay in heaven and hope that we somehow found our way to the Father. He left heaven and came to where we are to reveal the way to the Father (John 14:6). Too often our strategy for mission keeps us in the comfort of our worship services, Bible studies, and Christian comfort zones in the hope that sinners will somehow find their way in. I recently attended a Greenhouse Movement gathering where one of the speakers referred to Christians as being "Fishers of Men," even though too often this meant laying a net out on the beach and putting a sign up that reads, "FISH WELCOME". They won't just jump in! Fisher men and women have to actually go out into the water and let down their nets. Likewise, we must get out of our churches and go to where sinners are, just as Jesus left heaven and came to us. As he, so we…

Love Sinners

Why did Jesus come on his mission to save us? Because He loved us. John 3:16 is clear: "For God so loved the world, that he gave his only Son, that whoever believes in him should not perish but have eternal life" (ESV). God loved sinners enough to come to us in the person of the Son. And when He walked the earth, he practiced that love by associating with sinners. My favorite example is in Mark, chapter two, after Jesus chooses the tax collector, Levi, to be his disciple. "Later," it says, "Levi invited Jesus and his disciples to his home as dinner guests, along with many tax collectors and other disreputable sinners. (There were many people of this kind among Jesus' followers.) But when the teachers of religious law who were Pharisees saw him eating with tax collectors and other sinners, they asked his disciples, 'Why does he eat with such scum?' When Jesus heard this, he told them, 'Healthy people don't need a doctor—sick people do. I have come to call not those who think they are righteous, but those who know they are sinners'" (Mark 2:15-17 NLT). It is easy for Christians to slip into being more like the Pharisees and to see non-believers (or sinful Christians!) as scum rather than as Jesus did. He looked at sinners with love as lost sheep and entered into life with them to bring them salvation instead of the condemnation many of them already knew was hanging over their heads. As he, so we…

Practice Demonstration, Proclamation, and Transformation

Jesus' mission seemed to be a balance of these three. There would be some supernatural demonstration of the reality of God's Kingdom attached to the proclamation of the good news of God's Kingdom, followed by the transformation of the lives of those who believed. As Christ was sent to demonstrate, proclaim, and transform, so the disciples were sent to do the same. As you read the Book of Acts, they walked in that same balance throughout their mission. Just in Acts, chapter two, for example, you see the gift of other languages received (demonstration), Peter's bold address to the crowds (proclamation), and about 3,000 saved and the church formed (transformation). It continues in chapter three with the healing of the crippled beggar, and so on.

As he was sent, so we are sent. As we go out on mission, we can also expect the presence and power of the Holy Spirit to accompany our work. The Lord is willing to show that His Kingdom is real! The Spirit's work in and through us could be anything from acts of love and service to supernatural miracles. Of course, demonstration alone isn't enough, and there must also be a proclamation to explain how to enter God's Kingdom through repentance and belief in Jesus Christ. Finally, there must be transformation offered through being united to the Church and growing as a disciple through the continued work of the Holy Spirit. As he, so we . . .

Be "Yet" People

Jesus' ultimate mission was to give us new unending life through his incarnation, his sacrifice on the cross, and his resurrection from the dead. He left heaven to do this because he loved us, sinners though we are. It wasn't easy for him. In fact, at the moment before his crucifixion in the Garden of Gethsemane he asked the

Father for there to be another way (Matthew 26:39) but still prayed, "Yet not as I will, but as you will." There wasn't another way, so he did it anyway. As he was sent, so we are sent.

If we're honest, most of us really don't want to be sent on mission to do evangelism because much of it takes a lot of effort. It's hard even for people who are gifted at it! It would be nice if there was another way than for us to have to go out and do likewise. Of course, there isn't, so we must. The Church is God's "Plan A" for the Great Commission to be fulfilled on earth, and there is no "Plan B." As members of the Church, we each have our part to play, despite the difficulties that may come. We must accept that to be a sent people we must become a "yet" people. When we would rather not be on mission, we must pray as Jesus prayed: "Yet not as I will, but as you will." As he, so we . . .

CHAPTER 5:
STRUCTURAL RENEWAL

The fourth type of renewal that God takes a church through is structural renewal. When a church realizes it needs revitalization, it's usually already in the stage of decline, as can be seen in the Church Life Cycle diagram below.

The Church Life Cycle: Three Primary Stages

(used with permission of KenPriddy.com)

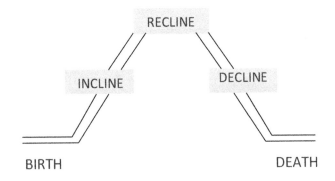

As opposed to a church in the Incline stage that is vision-driven, future-oriented, and focused on reaching the outside community, a church in Decline tends to be structure-driven, past-oriented, and focused on keeping the existing core members in place. Since a church in decline tends to be more focused on structures anyway, it makes sense that when they decide to work on revitalizing, their first instinct is to go straight to this fourth kind of renewal and skip the first three as mentioned in chapter one.

The thought is that if a few things here and there can be tweaked, everything will get better. If committees are reorganized and new people are put in charge, then growth will start again, or if a new and better sign is put out front, that will bring in young people with children. Or finally, a common quick organizational fix may be getting a new priest, pastor, or youth minister in order to fix the problems.

For these churches, it's especially important to remember that when God revitalizes a church, he takes them through all five types of renewal in order. Structural Renewal is not the place to start. Rather, it's a natural result of the first three types of renewal. When a congregation develops a real love for God (personal renewal), a real love for one another (relational renewal), and a real love for the lost (missional renewal), then it will get back to the Incline stage and grow again. As growth occurs, structural renewal is then needed to help maintain that growth.

One of the clearest biblical examples of this is in Acts, chapter six. The first three renewals happened in the previous chapters, and as a result, church growth happened. What worked structurally for the original 120 disciples, and then for the 3,000 disciples added at Pentecost, was not working anymore:

> "In those days when the number of disciples was increasing, the Hellenistic Jews among them complained against the Hebraic Jews because their widows were being overlooked in the daily distribution of food. So, the Twelve gathered all the disciples together and said, 'It would not be right for us to neglect the ministry of the word of God in order to wait on tables. Brothers and sisters, choose seven men from among you who are known to be full of the Spirit and wisdom. We will turn this responsibility over to them and will give our attention to prayer and the ministry of the word.' This proposal pleased the whole group. They chose Stephen, a man full of faith and of the Holy Spirit; also Philip, Procorus, Nicanor, Timon, Parmenas, and Nicolas from Antioch, a convert to Judaism. They presented these men to the apostles, who prayed and laid their hands on them. So, the word of God spread. The number of disciples in Jerusalem increased rapidly, and a large number of priests became obedient to the faith." (Acts 6:1-7 NIV)

Notice how, in the last two sentences, they didn't ignore the complaints of growth, collaboratively addressed the problem, and renewed their organizational structure, growth continued.

As your church is renewed and begins to grow again, you will find that what works with 20 members will not work with 50. What works with 50 will not work with 100. What works with 100 members will not work with 200, and so forth. Structural renewal will constantly need to be addressed for growth to continue. It won't cause growth, but it will maintain growth.

So how do you know if it's time to look at your church's structure and make the necessary changes for growth? There's a great quote from Dallas Willard that says, "Your current system is perfectly designed to get you the results you are getting." If you're stuck at 40, 70, or 200 members, it's likely that your current system is designed to allow only that many. Presupposing that your church has engaged (and continues to engage) the first three types of renewal, here are some structural renewal ideas that can be applied to your congregation:

Pay Attention to Complaints

Just as pain in my body is God's way of letting me know there is something wrong that needs to heal, complaining in a missional church can be an indication of a structural change that needs to be addressed. That was the case in Acts, chapter six, when the complaining led to an organizational change that allowed for more growth. It's true that sometimes people complain just to complain; then you have a character issue rather than a structural one. But it's worth taking the time to analyze the complaint to see if there is a legitimate "pain" occurring in the church body that God wants addressed for the congregation's greater health.

Be Willing to Change

If you are not willing to let go of "the way we've always done it," then you'll limit growth. This is why the first three renewals are required. If your relationship with God is so good that you are finding your identity and security in Him, conditions in the local church can change, and you'll still be okay! If you're looking to the local congregation, instead of Jesus, for your sense of security, you'll likely resist change in order to protect your sense of self. Similarly, if you love the lost, you'll do whatever it takes to reach even one more including bearing with any new change in structure that must happen whether it's difficult or not. Developing a culture of change in a growing church is an essential aspect of its renewal and growth.

Work Collaboratively Toward Solutions

American culture has changed so rapidly that things that worked even ten years ago are no longer relevant! Decades ago, when our culture was by and large more Christian, a church could "plug and play" the latest church growth model and see some success. Nowadays, however, none of us have it all figured out. There are no easy solutions or quick fixes for church growth in our times. As your church faces structural challenges, a collaborative approach is appropriate. In Acts, chapter six, it describes how the Twelve called the other leaders together to form a solution and that "this proposal pleased the whole group." This collaborative effort presupposes the Holy Spirit's involvement along with the apostles' leadership. A similar collaborative effort of the Holy Spirit, clergy, staff, and lay leaders (and sometimes even outside consultants) can bring to light the best solutions for your own church's problems. This collaborative process can reframe the problem to identify new ways forward. That is why the American Anglican Council calls our church consulting services Reframe Consulting.

Let Go of Control

Again, in the same section of Acts, the apostles modeled how to practice structural renewal when they said, "Brothers and sisters, choose seven men from among you who are known to be full of the Spirit and wisdom. We will turn this responsibility over to them…" The Twelve didn't try to do everything themselves! They knew their calling and delegated the rest of the necessary work.

In my first eight years of ordained ministry, I experienced an average of ten percent growth each year in two different congregations. In my ninth year, we didn't grow at all, and I was devastated. I brought in a consultant to address what I thought was a structural renewal issue. It was, and it turned out the issue was me! My unwillingness to delegate in several areas was bottlenecking our growth. I was even more devastated! However, I knew I loved my congregations and the community around me, so I decided to grapple with my own need for control and my unwillingness to let go. I had to reengage my own personal renewal and had to grow spiritually myself before the church could continue to grow. If you struggle to let go of control, I advise you to lean into the Lord through prayer and ask him to change that in you. Seek the counsel and prayers of wise leaders around you and pursue transformation until you see it take root in your heart. And then, just as the Apostles did, turn some of the church's responsibility over to wise, Spirit-filled, disciples.

CHAPTER 6:
CULTURAL RENEWAL

In this chapter I want to address the fifth and final renewal: Cultural Renewal. What is your ultimate reason for wanting your church to grow? Is it just to have a bigger church because bigger is better? Is it just not to close the doors if you don't grow? Is it just to maintain a legacy of Anglicanism in your community? Hopefully your ultimate reason for growing the local church is to fulfill the Great Commission and see God's Kingdom come, and his will be done, on earth as it is in Heaven.

God's Kingdom come is the great news of the Good News, that the Kingdom came through Jesus Christ so now Heaven can be experienced on earth, at least in part, until Jesus returns. Jesus' first public message after his baptism and temptation was this: "'The time has come,' he said. 'The kingdom of God has come near. Repent and believe the good news!'" (Mark 1:14b-15) Believe what good news? That the Kingdom of God has come near!

Establishing his kingdom is exactly what Jesus did

while bodily here on earth. And that is what he is continuing to do today, but now it is through the Holy Spirit in us, his body, the Church! The goal of every local church should not be to build up our own little kingdoms but to push back the kingdom of darkness on earth with God's rule and reign through Christ and his one Kingdom. We are to do that not only by seeing individual lives transformed, but, as a local expression of that Kingdom, seeing the culture around us transform.

In the American Anglican Council's Revive seminar, we ask the question, "If your church ceased to exist today, would anyone in your city/town (other than you) even notice?" Often the answer is no because the local church is not impacting the surrounding community and culture with the Good News in any meaningful way.

We believe that the local church is the hope of the world. If every local church fulfilled the unique part God wanted them to accomplish in transforming the culture around it, the culture of the whole world would be renewed! Every local church can't do everything, but every local church can do something. The Apostle Paul uses the image of the Body of Christ in 1 Corinthians 12 to describe how each individual has a part to play in the whole body of the local church, and in this case, that image would be appropriate for the entire Church where every local congregation can know it has a part in the workings of the greater whole. "If the whole body were an eye," Paul writes, "where would be the sense of hearing? If the whole body were an ear, where would be the sense of smell? But as it is, God arranged the members in the body, each one of them, as he chose. If all were a single member, where would the body be? As it is, there are many parts, yet one body." (1 Corinthians 12:17-20) If every local church on every local corner of every town or city in the world would discover and fulfill God's specific plan for them, the whole world would be transformed.

It's important to remember that this cultural renewal of transforming the community around our churches is the result of addressing and experiencing the other kinds of renewal first. After experiencing the personal renewal of the Holy Spirit on Pentecost, the relational renewal we read about in Acts 2:42-27, the missional renewal of thousands being saved through the early church's preaching, we then read about the whole city of Jerusalem being impacted by the Good News in Acts 5:26-28a (NLT): "The captain went with his Temple guards and arrested the apostles, but without violence, for they were afraid the people would stone them. Then they brought the apostles before the high council, where the high priest confronted them. 'We gave you strict orders never again to teach in this man's name!' he said. 'Instead, you have filled all Jerusalem with your teaching about him.'"

So what part is God calling your local church to play in bringing God's Kingdom to your local community? How can your congregation help bring a Christ-centered cultural renewal in your city/town? Here are some suggestions to get you going:

Believe the local church is the hope of the world

Your church, regardless of how big or small, is part of God's plan to transform your town or city. Believe it and don't settle for anything less than having a Kingdom of God impact in your culture.

Prayerfully identify your churches' specific part to renew your city/town

Be a student of your community. You live there. You know the people. You see the issues. What are the greatest needs? What are the needs no one is really addressing? Be specific to your particular part of town. What are the physical, spiritual, emotional, financial, relational needs not being met directly around your church? Based on the make-up of your church, how can you as a group best address those needs with God's help?

Our church was on the westside of the city. It was a depressed area but not as bad as the northside. People joked that the best part of the westside was that at least it wasn't the northside! We realized, though, that most of the government and non-profit help was found in the northside, while our side of town was being neglected. For example, there was nothing for addiction recovery in our area, so we decided to focus on that need in order to serve our community.

Do something

Once you've identified an area to bring Christ's influence, be the best church you have the capacity to be at meeting that need. It will take effort and decisive action, and it will need a lot of grace. Strive to become the church that the city would miss if you didn't do what you were called to do. Start small and let it develop. Just do something. At our church, we started a Christ-centered recovery ministry that in time became known as the go to church for people struggling with all sorts of addictions. If we closed, the people of the westside would feel it.

Take risks and expect to fail along the way

Not every good idea to meet the specific need that God reveals to you will work. Despite this reality, every experiment that fails is still a good education. What you learn through failures are the building blocks to landing on the right culture-renewing ministry God has for you. God wants to use your church to break forth his Kingdom into your community, and he has a plan for you to do it. Keep prayerfully moving forward until you find it, and then keep moving forward, improving as you go!

Partner with others

Sometimes, rather than having you start something new, God will show you a ministry already in town to partner with that is already doing what He is asking you to. Instead of reinventing the wheel, so to speak, you may be asked to come alongside this ministry or local church and add support to others.

Trust God

Trust God from the bottom of your heart, and don't try to figure out everything on your own. Listen for God's voice in everything you do, everywhere you go. He's the one who will keep you on track. As Jesus promised when he gave the Great Commission in Matthew 28, "And surely I am with you always, to the very end of the age" (Matt. 28:20 NIV). He is with you as you go!

CHAPTER 7:
GROWING OTHERS AS FAR AS YOU HAVE GROWN

One of my greatest frustrations over the years is how God always seems more interested in growing me than growing my church. I would have ongoing conversations with the Lord that sounded like this: "It's your church. You want people saved and discipled in your Kingdom more than me. Why are you so interested in my growth rather than the church's?" Although He has always given clear answers to my many questions over the course of my life, I don't ever remember a clear answer to this one! What did become clear, however, is that God's desire to grow me had a direct effect on my leadership, and, in turn, the spiritual and numerical growth of the church. As I noted in a previous chapter, when God worked on me, he was working on the "structures" of the church itself, bringing it renewal because as the congregation's leader I was a part of that structure.

I saw repeatedly that the healthier I became, the healthier the people I led became. I learned that you can only grow others as far as you have grown. You can't lead people where you haven't gone. You can point to and proclaim various spiritual truths from God's Word and be correct, but it's still not the same as speaking those truths from experience.

For example, I could preach and teach accurately on the necessity of our need to forgive others. I would use great lines often heard in recovery programs. "Unforgiveness is like drinking poison and hoping the other person gets sick." That was true and helpful to many, however, it wasn't until after I experienced serious betrayal both in the church and in my family that I could truly teach about genuine forgiveness. Having had to practice the forgiveness of deep hurts, I could more effectively help others offer forgiveness to those who wounded them.

In the same way, I was always a supporter of healing prayer ministries. I promoted them and encouraged many people to receive ministry for spiritual, emotional, and physical needs. We had an active healing ministry in the church. I would occasionally get prayer for a physical need myself, but I wasn't much into the emotional aspect of healing prayer. I knew it was good for others who had real problems, but I was "fine." I had a false belief that I couldn't show weakness as the church's leader. Stemming from the above-mentioned betrayals, I eventually came out of denial and realized I needed help, too. I ended up receiving emotional healing prayer and received significant breakthrough and freedom in Jesus. I became much more effective at helping others find similar freedom. Before encountering God in those places of pain, I only had head-knowledge about what He can do. When I combined that with an experience of the heart, however, the learning was much more powerful for those I led.

The same was true with giving. I always tithed because the Bible said to, and I didn't ever want to ask others to do something I wasn't willing to do myself. But I never considered myself a generous person. It's not that I gave a tithe grudgingly. I just saw it as my duty. I also believe that the ten percent belongs to God. So, tithing wasn't being generous with my money. The truth was that if God gave me 90% of my income (and kept the other ten percent), then true generosity for me would come from giving out of that 90%. I preached that generosity was greater than just a tithe and that you couldn't out-give God, but I was tight with my own 90%! I saw the discrepancy. I asked God to help me become more generous and then started increasing what I gave to more than just a tithe. Not surprisingly, I learned by experience that you can't out-give God. My ability to lead others in generous giving is now much more significant.

I could add to these experiences my own growth in loving others, in having peace about my Average Sunday Attendance figures, in the need to perform for approval from others, and much more, but I think you see the point here. As frustrated as I once was about God's greater interest in growing me than growing the church, I'm now very thankful that he was and is. Our own personal growth as leaders is often slow and painful, but it is worth it for our own soul and for the souls we have the honor to lead.

Where are you wanting to better grow and disciple

others? Would you be open to letting the Lord renew and grow you more in that area for both your and their sake? What areas of your spiritual, emotional, and physical life have you been resistant to the Lord's growing you? Perhaps God wants to give you a breakthrough so you can lead others to their breakthrough as well.

CHAPTER 8:
THE ZEAL OF REVITALIZATION

Someone recently told me that on New Year's Day, they always pick a word to be "their word" for the year. It never occurred to me to do that. However, last year I decided to try, and the word I chose was zeal.

Zeal is one of those words that seems to have dropped out of common use recently. I rarely, if ever, hear it used. One time I heard it was from an Anglican Archbishop, Ben Kwashi of Nigeria, when he was interviewed by Canon Phil Ashey of the American Anglican Council. When asked why the Anglican Church in Nigeria was so evangelistic, the archbishop talked about zeal. It caught my attention. I thought, "Right on! They still talk about zeal in Nigeria, and their churches are growing. Maybe we need more zeal if we are going to see our churches in North America revitalized."

So, what is zeal? The Dictionary.com app on my phone defines it as "fervor for a person, cause, or object; eager desire or endeavor; enthusiastic diligence; ardor."

The parts of that definition that apply to those seeking to grow local churches are "fervor for a person, cause" and "enthusiastic diligence." Wouldn't it be helpful if we all had both of those things for Jesus (a person) and the Great Commission (a cause)?

Normal "going through the motions" religion isn't going to grow any church. At best, it will maintain but even that's unlikely. Why would anyone who doesn't know Jesus want to come to your church if you aren't that excited about Jesus and his mission? I'm reminded of Jesus' words to the church in Laodicea: "I know your deeds, that you are neither cold nor hot. I wish you were either one or the other! So, because you are lukewarm—neither hot nor cold—I am about to spit you out of my mouth" (Rev. 3:15-16). Ouch! I suppose even though being cold is better than being lukewarm, I'd rather be hot. And what does hot mean? Zeal!

Being "on fire" for Jesus is contagious. And just in case you might believe being zealous is somehow improper for good Anglican Christians, a Collect (or prayer) for Mission in the Anglican prayer book reads like this:

Almighty and everlasting God, who alone works great marvels: Send down upon our clergy and congregations committed to their charge the life-giving Spirit of your grace, shower them with the continual dew of your blessing, and ignite in them a zealous love of your Gospel, through Jesus Christ our Lord. Amen (BCP 2019 pg. 24).

That's pretty good! It's a prayer for fire to be lit in us for Jesus and his Gospel. That's zeal!

Moving a church from maintenance to mission also takes diligence. There are no easy fixes or silver bullets.

It takes long, faithful diligence in the same Great Commission direction. Given the difficulties of revitalization, zeal gives us that fire in our bellies to persevere, to never quit for the sake of one more person coming to know Jesus Christ. In Luke 3:16, John the Baptist proclaimed that Jesus "will baptize you with the Holy Spirit and fire." What does "fire" mean in this passage? Certainly, it means the fire of judgment, a fire that refines and purges us of our sin. I would like to suggest that when the Spirit comes and brings fire, it also means bringing a supernatural zeal. In Christ, we not only receive the Holy Spirit's comfort, but we receive His power like a fire in us that fuels us onward. This supernatural zeal is a fire that burns within us and motivates us to stay diligent in fulfilling His Great Commission.

Would you ask the Lord to help you rediscover zeal? Would you pray and ask God to ignite in you a zealous love of Jesus and his Gospel? And then, let the fire inside of you give you the diligence to go and make disciples of the people around you that he has called you to reach!

CHAPTER 9:
TRUSTING GOD ENOUGH

The question of whether we trust God enough is an important one for any Christian, but it's essential for those pursuing church revitalization. As a church faces the challenges of becoming more missional, it takes a lot to trust in God. Do you trust that the one who created the entire universe from nothing is there to bring about His plans for you? Do you believe that He loves you and the people in your community, and that love sent his only Son to keep you from perishing and to gain eternal life? Do you believe He will come through for you now when you need Him?

I was recently struck by the profound truth in the first line of the Lord's Prayer: "Our Father, who art in Heaven..." God is a loving Father who cares deeply for us. He is also one who lives in Heaven which shows us his awesome power. He is both a loving and powerful God, both for us and with the power to help us. He wants our congregations to thrive more than we do. Do you trust him enough to help make that happen?

I remember when our church identified that God wanted us to reach certain people in our community living with lower incomes and whose lives were visibly broken. Biblically, we were excited. It seemed very Jesus-like! We were committed to reaching and making disciples of them because that's who lived around our church. Well, that's all great until questions about how we're going to pay for everything started coming in. Some members began voicing fear with comments like, "Maybe we should focus on reaching people with money because, you know, we have bills to pay," or "It's good to bring in these hurting people, Father Mark, but the existing members are going to have to carry the financial burden, and we don't have any wealthy people." There were other such comments.

I remember my own fearful thinking at the end of one membership class. One of the people joining our church was a formerly homeless crack addict. His girlfriend, who was also an addict and prostitute (when he occasionally sold her for drug money), had been coming to our church regularly because of our recovery ministry, and she had invited him to come and see. She kept telling him to try it because "this church is different." One Sunday morning despite his doubts, he decided to visit. That day's Bible reading included Matthew 8:20 in which Jesus says, "Foxes have dens and birds have nests, but the Son of Man has no place to lay his head" (NIV). When he heard that Jesus knew what it meant to be homeless, that was all it took for him to commit his life to Him and to join our church.

At the end of the membership class he attended,

he came up to me and said he forgot to put his offering in the plate during worship earlier that day and asked if he could just give it to me right there. He then proceeded to reach in his pocket and pull out a handful of change which he dumped into my cupped hands. Despite my pleasure at seeing this man's life being changed, I still couldn't help thinking, "How in the world are we going to pay our bills with this?!"

Did I really trust God enough? Around that time my Dad, who was a member of the church, shared with me what he believed the Lord had to say. "If you go after the ones nobody wants," he said, "God will give you the ones everybody wants." I hung onto that statement. I put my trust more deeply in our loving and powerful Father, and that he would provide what we needed. He did; every time.

And that formerly homeless crack addict who gave me his pocket change also taught himself to read using the Bible and ended up getting a job at a printing shop. After sharing his story with his new employer, the employer was so moved by the man's story that he gave our church a huge discount on our printing costs with his company. This ended up saving us thousands of dollars! God is so creative and so faithful.

Our all-powerful, all-loving God is for you and your church. He wants your church revived and to make a difference for his Kingdom in your community. He wants lives transformed through the ministry of your church. Despite the challenges of becoming a revitalized missional church, the struggle is worth it, and God is trustworthy. Do you trust him enough?

SECTION ONE DISCUSSION QUESTIONS
THE CORNERSTONE OF REVITALIZATION

1. Canon Mark describes that there is no church revitalization without renewal and that the renewals needed have an order: personal, relational, missional, structural, and cultural. Describe your response to this idea. Does it ring true to you? Have you experienced attempts at starting with structural renewals without first focusing on the first three? If so, how did that work?

2. Think about your own personal relationship with Jesus. Describe your current level of passion for Jesus in your own heart. If you need to renew your personal relationship with Jesus, what is one thing you will commit to doing this week to grow closer to him? If you are in a group, please share with the group your own story of salvation – when, where, and how did you come to know Jesus as your personal Lord and Savior?

3. Part of renewal in order to have revitalization is the need to be filled with the power of the Holy Spirit. Describe how have you experienced the presence and power of the Holy Spirit in your life.

4. Think about the love you have for one another in your local church. Describe how authentic love for each other is expressed. If you would say that there needs to be relational renewal in your church, what is one thing your church could commit to do over the next six weeks to grow in this area? If you are in a group, please share with the group a time when you experienced genuine love and care from a member of your church family.

5. Think about the love your local church has for lost, or unchurched, people outside your congregation. Do you know who the specific unchurched people around your church are that God wants you to "Go" to fulfill the Great Commission? Who are you "sent" to specifically? What will you commit to doing over the next six weeks to identify them and begin to develop a strategy to go to reach them?

6. Please describe a time when God has renewed and transformed you in order to better love and serve others. Be as vulnerable as you are comfortable.

7. Do you trust God enough? Please describe a time when you have seen God come through for you in an amazing way. What might you try out of

your comfort zone in order to revitalize your church?

SECTION TWO:
A GREAT COMMITMENT TO THE GREAT COMMISSION

Therefore, go and make disciples of all nations, baptizing them in the name of the Father and of the Son and of the Holy Spirit, and teaching them to obey everything I have commanded you. And surely, I am with you always, to the very end of the age. Matthew 28:19-20 (NIV)

Again, Jesus said, "Peace be with you! As the Father has sent me, I am sending you."
John 20:21 (NIV)

CHAPTER 10:
A HOSPITAL FOR SINNERS

I had the privilege of attending a course on Church Revitalization at Gordon Conwell Theological Seminary in Hamilton, Massachusetts. One of the presenters, Dr. Jim Singleton, gave a very good, succinct summary of the challenge our churches face in North America. He described how we are living in a time of transition in our formerly Christian culture that requires a different church response. We moved from a "Christendom" period in the mid 1900's, where most of the culture was Christian or at least adhered to Christian morality, to a "Missional" period, where the culture is not mostly Christian and sometimes against expressions of faith. This new period is distasteful to many of us who grew up in that age of American Christendom; we don't like it.

As I pondered this reality and our need for revitalization in North America, I thought of the adage, "The Church is a hospital for sinners, not a hotel for saints." Though we all probably agree with this concept, the truth is that for those of us who grew up in Christendom, the Church as hotel for saints worked just fine. That more accurately describes our experience in church. The Church must see herself as a hospital for sinners and making that shift in mindset is hard.

We know how to be a hotel. We know how to set things up to look nice for existing Christians to come in, be comfortable, and enjoy our services. We don't know how to set up an emergency room or a recovery ward where we nurse hurting, broken individuals who are either unchurched non-Christians or wounded, lost Christians in need of real help to get back on track. Many in our society no longer know how to even behave in a church, and we don't know how to show them. We didn't have to before, and no one taught us how because we were in a culture where most people (at least on the outside) weren't claiming to be sick but to be saints.

In the Christendom culture that many of us grew up in, most people identified as Christians and learned how to be "good" primarily in their homes. In many parts of the country, the community and the church were almost synonymous. The church was just a place for gathering the existing Christians in the community for worship and fellowship. Like choosing between hotels, Christians would pick a church that suited their preferences. One hotel has stained glass, and the other doesn't; another has guitar music, while another plays only organ music. If some believers liked their hotel better, that was fine, as long as everyone had a hotel to go to. Well, in most places around America, those days are gone. The reality is that those who identify as Christian are in strong decline, and those who are devout, regular church-attendees are no longer in the majority.

Revitalization will require us to confront this new reality by becoming the missional church that our times call for and our culture desperately needs. The word mission means "to be sent," or better, "to be propelled out." We must learn how to get outside our church walls and connect with those who are sick, and, like first responders, bring them into the Church as a hospital to find the healing only Jesus and His people can provide. This is the kind of church Jesus calls us to be anyway. In John 20:21 when Jesus first appeared to his disciples after the resurrection, he said to them, "Peace be with you. As the Father has sent me, even so I am sending you" (ESV). As He was sent to save sinners, to find the sick and heal them, even so we are sent on mission to do the same.

Jesus' missional style was also a change for the people in Palestine all those centuries ago. The religious leaders of the day preferred a "hotel for saints" model, too. Mark, chapter 2, is a prime example of this attitude. When Jesus was spending his time building relationships with sinners outside of the temple, the scribes and the Pharisees wondered why he was with "those people." It says:

> "Many tax collectors and sinners were reclining with Jesus and his disciples, for there were many who followed him. And the scribes of the Pharisees, when they saw that he was eating with sinners and tax collectors, said to his disciples, 'Why does he eat with tax collectors and sinners?' And when Jesus heard it, he said to

> them, 'Those who are well have no need of a physician, but those who are sick. I came not to call the righteous, but sinners.'" (Mark 2:15-17 ESV)

Jesus' answer to their question implied that the church is supposed to be a hospital for sinners, not a hotel for saints. His own mission was to those who knew they were sick in order to bring them healing.

Here is a good question to honestly ask yourself: Is the leadership in my church acting like hotel clerks or like hospital nurses? Is my church more of a hotel for saints or a hospital for sinners? If your answer is more "hotel," then know you are not alone. Many churches, Anglican ones included, are unconsciously hanging onto the "Christendom" age wanting the way we've always done things to still work. If we were still in "Christendom," it would still be working. In recovery programs, the first step to healing is admitting there is a problem. The first step to revitalization is admitting Christendom is over and that we have a problem. I'm sure there is someone reading this right now who thinks that to become more of a hospital means giving up what they love about their own Christian traditions. That's not true. You can be both Anglican and still be missional. You can have an Anglican church for the unchurched.

Here are three steps to begin:

1. Admit that Christendom is over and that wishing for its return won't bring it back.
2. Believe that it's possible to be Anglican (or whatever other Christian tradition you come from) and still be missional.

3. Commit to doing whatever it takes for your church to become a hospital for sinners.

CHAPTER 11:

LETTING THE VISION DRIVE
THE DECISION

Vision is so often a part of the discussion when trying to bring health and growth to a local church and rightly so. One of the sessions in our Revive seminar is dedicated to vision and core values. But why is having a clear, well-defined, and memorable vision so important to church health? That's what this chapter will address.

Anyone who has served in local-church leadership has heard of vision statements. Many a governing board has hammered one out and printed it somewhere, maybe even in the weekly bulletin. Often, not much is ever done with it. When I speak on church revitalization, it is often the case that no one even remembers their vision statement. I've heard many church leaders dismiss them as a waste of time despite their importance. The problem is that they are not utilized the way they need to be to produce health and growth.

The church's vision should drive every decision the church makes. Think about the hundreds of decisions a local church has to make every year:

- *Should we spend money on this or that?*
- *Mrs. New Idea wants us to start this new program. Should we?*
- *Mr. Liturgy insists we add or remove some part of the Sunday service. Should we?*
- *Should we change the style of music?*
- *Should we do Alpha or Christianity Explored or Celebrate Recovery or Rooted or another program or none of them at all?*
- *Should we keep doing both Sunday School and Children's Church?*
- *Should we add a staff member?*
- *Should we use name tags?*
- *Should we…?*

The decision for these and every other question that arises should be filtered through the specific vision your church has committed to. That vision must, of course, grow out of God's vision for the Church expressed in the Bible. When any question comes up, the very next question should be, "Does it help us fulfill our vision or not?" If not, then don't do it. Even if it's a perfectly good thing for a church to do, if it doesn't fit the agreed upon vision, it's not for your church. Don't do it.

Part of a vision's beauty is that it gives leadership a standard to base decisions on. Rather than being at the mercy of the rector, vestry, or largest contributor's whims, the vision is what drives all decisions. If a decision is based on the vision, then blame can fall on the vision rather than the leadership. If the answer based on the vision to moving forward in a direction is yes, then the time, talent, and treasure of the church can be given to it because the agreed upon vision needs it.

At my last church, our vision was to have a Great Commitment to the Great Commandment and the Great Commission (and to be honest, we happily stole it from another church!). It's a biblical and memorable statement, but it was still not specific enough to our local context. So based on that initial statement, we narrowed it down to answer how to fulfill that vision, specifically, in our local community. We determined that our more specific vision was to focus on the many lower income families around us, and we saw how many of them wouldn't come to church if invited because although they believed in God, they assumed He wanted to punish them. We chose to zero in on this particular "people group" in our part of world which is exactly what we are called to do in the Great Commission. We described this more specific vision in terms of seeing these folks whose lives were visibly broken changed for good by Jesus and his church. Our slogan for that became, "A Church Where Lives Are Changed for Good!" This clearer, more specific vision then became the filter for our decision-making.

Question: Should we do a contemporary worship service? Will that better help us reach, love, and make disciples of the people group we're committed to reaching? **Answer:** Yes. Let's do it.

Question: Should we invest in doing Alpha because that's been successful for evangelism in other

Anglican churches? Will doing the Alpha program better help us reach, love, and make disciples of this people group?

Answer: No. They're more worried about not having a job and coping with their addictions than in attending a program that answers, "the bigger questions of life." Alpha may be a very good program, but it's not for our church in this season of our life together. So, if not Alpha, what would we do? We decided on Celebrate Recovery, a Christ-centered, 12-Step Ministry which we thought would connect better to those around us. It worked well.

Question: Should we make all the new people smoking in front of the church stop smoking? Long-time, faithful, non-smoking members were having to walk through clouds of smoke to come into the church and were appropriately unhappy about it. Since our vision is to reach and bring in a people group full of smokers (and who have made good progress in leaving behind other more damaging vices like crack cocaine), should we tell them they can't smoke in front of the church? Should we make it an issue?

Answer: Yes and No. The vision-driven decision was to create a designated smoking area off to the side of the church and hang a sign that said, "'Tis better to smoke in this life than in the next!" All involved were happy with the decision, those who were smokers were not unnecessarily offended or driven away, the long-time members didn't have to walk through smoke on their way into church, and the vision the see "lives changed for good" kept going.

So, what is your church's clear, biblical, memorable, and specific vision? It's not enough to just have it on the bulletin cover, website, or in your church by-laws. Dust it off, narrow it down, know it, and start using that vision to drive every decision.

CHAPTER 12:
COMMUNICATING THE COMMISSION

You're no doubt familiar with the saying that the three most important things in real estate are "Location, Location, Location." Similarly, it seems the three most important things when it comes to trying to motivate a congregation to become missional are "Communication, Communication, Communication."

Church Revitalization is hard. The longer a church is plateaued or in decline and the older the members, the longer it will take to get it growing again. Revitalization takes time and is often a slower process than those of us who are passionate about it would like. I've talked with many a frustrated church leader, both lay and clergy, who just can't understand why more people aren't on board with becoming missional.

Since you are reading this book, you are likely a church leader longing to see the church revitalized. Let me encourage you not to devalue the long-term effectiveness of communication. Communicating the Great

Commission a lot, over time, is effective in turning around a church's internal culture.

I wrote earlier that one of the leadership clichés I've regularly relied on is, "You get more of what you focus on." When I'd focus my communication on ministry, more people got involved in ministry. When I focused on small groups, more people got into small groups. And the more I focused on being missional, the more people became missional. One of the main ways of focusing on a subject is by communicating it, in addition to practicing whatever it is you are teaching about. So, if you want to see your church revitalized to better fulfill the Great Commission, communicate, communicate, communicate the commission!

And communication is not just from the pulpit. There are other ways to communicate the Great Commission effectively:

Pray

Prayer is obviously more than a communication tool, but it does communicate. Enlist an intercessory prayer team to pray for church revitalization and local mission. As they gather or spread your prayer requests to others, your heart for revitalization gets communicated. Host prayer events where church members can gather to pray for the lost in the community by name if you know them. Pray for evangelistic outreach programs in the corporate prayers that occur during the service. Encourage people to identify and pray for non-believers that they know personally. These are just some ideas. How else could you utilize prayer to communicate the Great Commission in your congregation?

The best part about this strategy is that in prayer you are primarily communicating to God, and He will act in response. Remember, he wants your church to grow and people to be saved more than you do. In Luke 15:5-7, Jesus gives the parable about finding the lost sheep. He says, "And when he has found it, he will joyfully carry it home on his shoulders. When he arrives, he will call together his friends and neighbors, saying, 'Rejoice with me because I have found my lost sheep.' In the same way, there is more joy in heaven over one lost sinner who repents and returns to God than over ninety-nine others who are righteous and haven't strayed away!" (NLT)

Preach

If you are clergy and regularly preach, the pulpit is a powerful communication tool. One or two sermons here and there on the Great Commission won't transform the congregation's culture. Many church members grew up in what I referred to earlier as Christendom, a culture that was sufficiently Christian so that we didn't have to be missional for a church to be "successful." Those days are gone. Church revitalization requires all Christians to realize there won't be enough people who wander into our church doors anymore to keep up with or exceed the members who die or move away. Unless the congregation transitions to being missional, it will eventually shrink and die. That needs to be communicated, communicated, communicated. Yes, you should also preach on worship, discipleship, ministry, stewardship, fellowship, etc., but when you need change in a certain area, focus on that area at least for a season. Preach the Great Commission. A lot.

Promote

What I mean here is the utilization of all the various communication tools churches have. Communicate the importance of the Great Commission through bulletins, newsletters, e-newsletters, bulletin boards, social media, presentations before, during, and after worship, and whatever other creative ways you can think of. I've often heard repeated the idea that people must read or hear something at least seven times before it registers. My own experience in ministry seems to validate that statement.

Practice

Giving people opportunities to experience local mission and evangelism is far more transformative than only preaching and promoting it. Early on in our revitalization efforts, we did a 40-day campaign with the theme, "Deepening the Community in the Church and Reaching the Community Outside the Church." We challenged everyone to join a small group and for each group to participate in a church outreach. Those groups ended up coming together to replace and completely furnish a wheelchair-bound widow's mobile home including building her a ramp. The entire congregation got so caught up in the project and received so much joy from serving outside the church walls, that local mission was no longer a question of "Should we be missional?" but "When can we be missional again?"! That experience was a catalyst for the missional culture the congregation developed more fully later. What missional experience can you create to let people put into practice the Great Commission in your community?

CHAPTER 13:
MOTIVATION MATTERS

Imagine your church is declining and in danger of closing. Would you want to help save it? Why would you want to? Is it because you love your church family and want that family to have a church home? Is it because you're attached to the building, a place you've invested so much in and don't want to see empty or sold? Is it because you love your tradition and want it to be available to your community? Those are all good reasons, but they aren't the best reasons for saving a dying church. If those are your primary motivators, you will eventually lose your church.

Any foundational reason other than advancing the Gospel and making disciples is the wrong reason to save a dying church. If you want to preserve your church family, your buildings that you've sacrificed for, or your Anglican presence in your community, you must give them up as the primary motivators for mission. These may be factors; however, they can't be the main motivator.

Matthew 16:23-25 (NLT) tells us, "Jesus turned to

Peter and said, 'Get away from me, Satan! You are a dangerous trap to me. You are seeing things merely from a human point of view, not from God's.' Then Jesus said to his disciples, 'If any of you wants to be my follower, you must give up your own way, take up your cross, and follow me. If you try to hang on to your life, you will lose it. But if you give up your life for my sake, you will save it.'"

You may have heard sermons on taking up our cross and the need to die to self, but have you ever thought to apply this principle to your local church? To put it another way, if you try to hang on to your physical church, you will lose it. But if you give it up and give it over to Jesus, you will save it. It's one of those frustrating spiritual truths we must embrace. If we try so hard to hang on to and grow our churches for our own sake, we will lose them. If in trying to save your church, your church becomes more important to you than Jesus, you will lose it. If liturgy is more important to you than Jesus, you will lose it. If being Anglican is more important to you than Jesus, you will lose it. However, if you give up your church, letting it and its growth go into the hands of Jesus and put your relationship with Jesus first, you will end up saving it.

As a reminder, if revitalization is to happen in any congregation, there must first be an ongoing personal renewal in the hearts of everyone in it. The clergy must love and follow Jesus more than the congregation they lead. The laity must love and follow Jesus more than the building, the history, the tradition, or whatever else. Personal renewal always precedes other kinds of renewal, and this sets a good foundation and motivation for our mission.

In my first position as an associate priest in

Midland, Texas, I was hired to implement church growth strategies primarily from The Purpose Driven Church, by Rick Warren. This was before his more famous book, The Purpose Driven Life, came out. In the three years I was at that church, it went from around 180 to over 330 members in attendance every Sunday. I thought, "This church growth stuff is easy!" It wasn't until I became rector of a long-time plateaued church in need of revitalization that I realized the success I experienced in Midland was based on the years of personal renewal that took place in that congregation prior to my arrival. The congregation experienced such a personal renewal of love for Jesus, primarily through the Alpha Program, that they were compelled to do whatever it took to reach more people with the Gospel. I was hired after that personal renewal took place to help make their desire for missional renewal happen, and I got to enjoy the harvest of their years of sowing the seeds of renewal.

As a new rector in that plateaued church I quickly realized I wasn't going to have the luxury I enjoyed in Midland and that I had to start from scratch. Eventually, the Lord led that church deeper into relationship with Him, too, and revitalization began there. To be clear, we didn't wait until a magical time when everyone in the congregation was fully in love with Jesus in order to start making important strategic changes, but over time as the congregation matured in their personal faith, they began to express the Great Commission ahead of other important goals and revitalization accelerated. Personal renewal preceded congregational and missional renewal.

So, what is your motivation for church

revitalization? Is it to save your church? Or is it that you are so in love with Jesus that you're compelled to fulfill his mission, whatever it takes? Is Jesus first and most important to you in all things, even more important than your church? Do you look to Jesus for peace and security more than your congregation, and is his mission to establish the Kingdom a more important motivation than any other mission you may have? If so, you're well on your way to revitalizing your church.

CHAPTER 14:
MEETING MORE NEEDS (WITHOUT MORE MEETINGS ABOUT MEETING MORE NEEDS)

Have you ever been in a church meeting on the need for evangelism and then see that nothing ever came of it? There's lots of talking and some good ideas, but there's no follow up, no evangelism, and no growth. If you've been active in the Church for even a little while, chances are you've experienced this. I once heard a speaker say, "The Church should have fewer meetings about meeting needs and just meet more needs!" Amen! Wouldn't it be great if we stopped talking about it and started doing it? Some attempt at evangelism would be better than more meetings that end up going nowhere.

If none of us like unproductive meetings, then why are such meetings so common? Why do we talk about the need for evangelism yet never do anything about it? There are certainly many reasons, fear being one of them, but a primary reason is that deep down we just don't really want to do evangelism even though we know we should. Talking about evangelism makes us feel a little less guilty about not doing anything because we think, "At least I went to that meeting!"

Do we really care enough to serve people in our community and share the Gospel with them? Sure, we want the Church to grow. Sure, we want young families in the Church. Sure, we want people to go to Heaven when they die. Or do we? Do we forget that without Jesus people are cut off from a relationship with God and are stumbling through darkness unable to turn their lives around now and that eventually leads to Hell? Do we forget to really care about them?

There are three principals that can be applied to counter this common apathy towards action:

Restore

Can you recall the moment you crossed from death to life and went from not knowing God to having a relationship with Him? Even those who have always believed in God can usually recall a moment when their faith became real to them and not just something they were raised with. Psalm 51:12 (ESV) says, "Restore to me the joy of your salvation, and uphold me with a willing spirit." Ask God to restore that joy you had when you first came to know Him. Restoring that joy in your heart will cause you to want others to experience it, too. Restore your joy in the Lord.

Remember

These words from Jesus to the church in Ephesus may be particularly appropriate to many Christians today: "I know your works, your toil and your patient endurance, and how you cannot bear with those who are evil, but have tested those who call themselves apostles and are not, and found them to be false. I know you are enduring patiently and bearing up for my name's sake, and you have not grown weary. But I have this against you, that you have abandoned the love you had at first. Remember therefore from where you have fallen; repent and do the works you did at first. If not, I will come to you and remove your lampstand from its place, unless you repent" (Rev. 2:2-5 ESV). Many Anglicans today have fought hard for Biblical truth. That is a very good thing. But we must still remember to maintain our love for Jesus with everything we have. If you lose that first love, you'll lose the desire to share Him with others as well. Press into your relationship with Jesus Christ. Remember your first love in order to keep your vision for mission to others fresh and alive.

Receive

Sometimes we might be too tired to do one more thing. That's because we've used up all our energy going to meetings! Effective evangelism is dependent on the power of the Holy Spirit, and even the disciples were told not to try it on their own. Jesus initially said to wait: "But you will receive power when the Holy Spirit has come upon you, and you will be my witnesses in Jerusalem and in all Judea and Samaria, and to the end of the earth" (Acts 1:8 ESV). When the Holy Spirit did come on Pentecost after they waited, evangelism happened, and the church grew. Have you received the Spirit's power? Have you asked to be filled up in order to be poured out for others? If not, then perhaps meeting about meeting needs is all you have the power to do! Pray and ask the Holy Spirit to come and fill you with His power to do more, to serve people around you, and to witness to them about Jesus Christ. Receive the Holy Spirit.

CHAPTER 15:
BELIEVING FOR COURAGE

Having a vision for and fulfilling the Great Commission takes courage. It requires leading the Church through change, and whenever there's change, there's loss. Whenever there's loss, there's pain. This pain often appears in the congregation as conflict. It's a fearful thing to make decisions that will cause people pain and conflict. Courage steps in to help push you through. It isn't the absence of fear but the overcoming of the obstacle in front of you despite your fear.

So, how do we gain this courage? Jesus tells us right in the Great Commission itself. He will be with us, even to the end of the age:

> Then Jesus came to them and said, "All authority in heaven and on earth has been given to me. Therefore, go and make disciples of all nations, baptizing them in the name of the Father and of the Son and of the Holy Spirit, and teaching them to obey everything I have

commanded you. And surely, I am with you always, to the very end of the age." Matthew 28:18-20 (NIV)

During a time when we were clarifying our vision to strategically reach the unchurched in our neighborhood, there was a lot of pushback from some members. The unchurched people were different in so many ways: in culture, income level, and personal struggles. Essentially, it meant bringing in "sinners" whose lives were openly broken. To reach them meant doing some things differently than what we were used to. It meant change. This meant pain for some of the members. Their pain led to anxiety in the whole congregation and resulted in some people leaving or threatening to leave. And when/if they left, they left with their money! It was a fearful time for me as a priest. I needed courage.

During that time, the deacon serving at the church gave me a plaque that said, "Courage" on top with Joshua 1:9 written below which says, "Be strong and courageous. Do not be afraid; do not be discouraged, for the Lord your God will be with you wherever you go" (NIV) Believing God was with me and drawing courage from that reality, we made the necessary changes. The church not only survived the ensuing conflict but thrived. To this day, I keep that plaque by my desk as a constant reminder that the courage needed comes from believing that the Lord is with me.

Look at what the Bible tells us in Isaiah 41:10 (NIV): "So do not fear, for I am with you; do not be dismayed, for I am your God. I will strengthen you and help you; I will uphold you with my righteous right hand."

The question for us as we face our fears is if we really believe in the core of our being whether this is true. Is he really with me to strengthen and help me?

What are you afraid of? Is knowing that Jesus is with you not enough to overcome those fears? If not, why not? Do you question whether God will come through to strengthen, help, and uphold you? What else do you think you need? The approval of people? The absence of conflict?

The answers to these questions are not easily discerned sometimes, however, they are essential answers to find in order to understand what you need from God as a leader in the Church. As an Anglican priest, most of my help reflecting on this came from having a good mentor and through clergy accountability groups where I could openly explore these answers among safe people and in a safe environment. The American Anglican Council provides excellent opportunities for both individual coaching and clergy accountability groups (visit our website to find out more: www.americananglican.org), and there may be other ways of finding these opportunities in your own local context. It's worth pursuing. For now, I want to encourage you to take some personal time to reflect privately on the answers to those questions, and to see what may be keeping you from having courage in the face of difficulty, or what you may need in the coming months as you seek to fulfill the Great Commission in your own church.

And never forget that in the same Great Commission we are called to fulfill, which is not easy, Jesus himself promised he'd be right there doing it with us saying, "And surely I am with you always, to the very end of the age" Matthew 28:20 (NIV).

SECTION TWO DISCUSSION QUESTIONS
A GREAT COMMITMENT TO THE GREAT COMMISSION

1. Prior to reading this book, were you familiar with the differences between what was described as "Christendom" in the past and the "Missional Church" that is now called for? Please describe your experience of being equipped to be on mission (or do evangelism).

2. Canon Mark described the need for a Great Commitment to the Great Commission. Please read all five versions of Jesus' commission and describe common themes (Matthew 28:16-20; Mark 16:15; Luke 24:46-49; John 20:21; Acts 1:8). What are some ways your church could put into practice this commission more effectively?

3. Does your church have a vision statement? What is it? Is it clear, specific, doable? To your

knowledge does your congregation let this vision drive every decision? If applicable, describe an experience in church where not having clarity and unity on the congregation's vision led to conflict and confusion.

4. What do you think is your primary motive for wanting to revive your church? What do you think is the primary motive for others in your church?

5. Do you agree or disagree with Canon Mark's assertion that anything less than a deep love for Jesus and a commitment to obey his commission to go and make disciples won't be enough to revive the church? Please explain.

SECTION THREE:

INSISTING ON CHURCH HEALTH

They devoted themselves to the apostles' teaching and to the fellowship, to the breaking of bread and to prayer. Everyone was filled with awe, and many wonders and miraculous signs were done by the apostles. All the believers were together and had everything in common. Selling their possessions and goods, they gave to anyone as he had need. Every day they continued to meet together in the temple courts. They broke bread in their homes and ate together with glad and sincere hearts, praising God and enjoying the favor of all the people. And the Lord added to their number daily those who were being saved.
Acts 2:42-47

CHAPTER 16:
HEALTH VERSUS GROWTH

If your church has maintained or declined in attendance, you probably want it to grow. You probably wouldn't be reading this book if you didn't want your church to grow! In this case, the first question most people ask is, "How can we get our church to grow?" We believe that is the wrong first question.

The right first question is, "How can we get our church to be healthy?" You see, the Church is the Body of Christ, as it says in 1 Corinthians 12:27 (NLT), "All of you together are Christ's body, and each of you is a part of it." The church is a body, not a business. It is a living organism, not just an organization. Living things, if healthy, naturally grow. Plants are a good simple example. Plants don't grow by telling them to grow or by hoping they grow. They grow by keeping them healthy. When healthy, they naturally grow as God designed them to grow. In the same way, your local church will grow if you focus on its care, on keeping it healthy.

So how can you foster health? The answer is by doing what Jesus told the Church to do! He summarized what He wants us to do in both the Great Commandment and the Great Commission. In these two scriptures, we find the five vital principles that every church must put into practice in order to be healthy and grow. Just as the human body has multiple systems that fulfill different functions, we are only healthy when all the systems work properly and in balance together. If all systems but one work well, you're still unhealthy. Likewise, if all five of these vital areas are working together as God designed them to, the Church will be healthy and grow. If one or two areas are off, it won't.

The good news is that every church already works in all five vital areas in some way. The bad news is that most local churches are strong in one or two areas and not in the others and are, therefore, unhealthy. All five areas must be engaged in a balanced way.

In the American Anglican Council's Revive Seminar, we have put these five vital areas into the acrostic, VITAL so they are easy to remember. They are:

VISION FOR MISSION:

From the Great Commission, "Go . . ." This means both personal evangelism and the church's missional strategy as a whole.

INTENTIONAL WORSHIP:

From the Great Commandment, "You shall love the Lord your God..." This means that as you gather to express your love for God in worship, you do so keeping in mind how visiting non-believers would experience every aspect of before, during, and after your worship service.

TRANSFORMATIONAL DISCIPLESHIP:

From the Great Commission, "Teaching them to observe all that I have commanded you . . ." This means to have a spiritual formation process in place that moves people from unchurched to fully mature and missional followers of Jesus. In other words, have a plan to "make disciples".

AUTHENTIC COMMUNITY:

From the Great Commission, "Baptizing them…" This means to bring people into union with Christ and His people, a genuine community of believers where individuals can belong, be loved, and be transformed.

LAY MOBILIZATION:

From the Great Commandment, "You shall love your neighbor…" This means having a plan to help every member discover who God made them to be so they can fulfill what he made them to do, both inside and outside the church.

Every church already dabbles in all five of these areas (or, at least, four of these areas with a committee to talk about doing evangelism!). Churches have been engaging these areas of Kingdom life for 2,000 years and will continue to do so until Jesus returns. So, the issue is not finding what we have to do. The issue is doing what we already know we're supposed to do and to do it with excellence in a balanced way.

CHAPTER 17:
KEY ASPECTS OF GROWING YOUR CHURCH

It's impossible to fully grasp all that happened when the Holy Spirit was poured out on the Day of Pentecost; however, I'd like to draw your attention to two events that took place that day - a demonstration of God's glory followed by a proclamation of God's gospel. These two things went together throughout the rest of the book of Acts and have gone together ever since. Believers, filled with the Holy Spirit, demonstrate God's glory in various ways. Non-believers take notice and ask, "What's this all about?" Then there's an opportunity for the proclamation God's Gospel. People get saved.

In Acts 2:12 after the Holy Spirit came upon the disciples, and they spoke in the languages of the people around them, it says, "Amazed and perplexed, they [the non-believers] asked one another, 'What does this mean?'" (NIV) Good question. Rather than leave them to wonder or figure it out on their own, the disciples used words to explain it. In Acts 2:14, Peter "stood up with the Eleven, raised his voice and addressed the crowd: 'Fellow Jews and all of you who live in Jerusalem, let me explain this to you; listen carefully to what I say.'" (NIV) He proclaimed the Gospel and many repented and believed and were saved. The demonstration of God's glory led to the proclamation of God's gospel. May we, in the power of the Spirit, do the same in our day!

With three thousand new believers added to the Church on that day, the first local church was formed. Through them, we see a wonderful snapshot of what God intended for his church to be and do:

> "They devoted themselves to the apostles' teaching and to the fellowship, to the breaking of bread, and to prayer. Everyone was filled with awe, and many wonders and miraculous signs were done by the apostles. All the believers were together and had everything in common. Selling their possessions and goods, they gave to anyone as he had need. Every day they continued to meet together in the temple courts. They broke bread in their homes and ate together with glad and sincere hearts, praising God and enjoying the favor of all the people. And the Lord added to their number daily those who were being saved." (Acts 2:42-47 NIV)

Can you see the five vital aspects of a healthy church that were introduced in the last chapter described in that passage? What they did wasn't over-complicated, and it is what every local church has done ever since. When a congregation balances these same five areas, it will be healthy, and healthy congregations will grow. In this first church, we see people who are in love with Jesus and filled with the Holy Spirit doing these same five things:

1. **Gathering for regular Worship:** "Every day they continued to meet together in the temple courts." (v. 46) This was for corporate worship. They gathered daily. We at least gather weekly.

2. **Meeting together for Fellowship:** "They broke bread in their homes and ate together with glad and sincere hearts, praising God and enjoying the favor of all the people" (v .46) describes the small groups wherever those three thousand lived and describes the common meal they shared in their fellowship.

3. **Growing in Discipleship:** "They devoted themselves to the apostles' teaching and to the fellowship, to the breaking of bread, and to prayer." (v. 42) They studied, learned, and practiced what they received from the apostles, and they grew to maturity as followers of the risen Christ.

4. **Serving in Ministry:** "Everyone was filled with awe, and many wonders and miraculous signs were done by the apostles. All the believers were together and had everything in common. Selling their possessions and goods, they gave to anyone as he had need." (v. 43-45) These Christians used their gifts to serve the church family and gave generously of their time, talents, and treasure.

5. **Bringing others into the Church:** "And the Lord added to their number daily those who were being saved." (v. 47) Through demonstrating God's glory in signs and wonders and in their unique love for one another, the Church continuously proclaimed the Gospel to those who witnessed their way of life. People were saved. The church grew numerically and began to spread.

If you want your church to grow, these five ways of living church life are necessary. It's not complicated; however, it's not exactly easy either. Staying focused on all five VITAL principles of healthy growing churches (Vision for Mission, Intentional Worship, Transformational Discipleship, Authentic Community, Lay Mobilization) is key to knowing whether or not your church is moving in the right direction, staying in balance, and being a healthy local church that will grow.

SECTION THREE DISCUSSION QUESTIONS
INSISTING ON CHURCH HEALTH

1. How is your church doing in all five of these vital areas? Describe how you are engaging them all.
2. Are you doing them all well or are there one or two areas you think you are stronger? Which ones are those, and why do you think that is the case?
3. What is your church's current plan for each VITAL area? How is your local congregation living out these same five areas that the first local congregations did?
4. How can you foster a balanced approach to engaging all five well (Don't worry if you don't have a lot of ideas at this point)?

Note: If you would like to have a quantitative analysis of your congregation's overall church health, you can take the Revive Church Health Assessment which we offer in partnership with Asbury

Seminary. You can access this assessment tool at www.churchrevive.org for a cost of only $100 for the entire congregation to participate.

SECTION 4:
VITAL STRATEGIES
FOR REVITALIZATION

When I am with those who are weak, I share their weakness, for I
want to bring the weak to Christ. Yes, I try to find common ground
with everyone, doing everything I can to save some.
1 Corinthians 9:22 (NLT)

PART 1:
VISION FOR
EVANGELISM AND MISSION

CHAPTER 18:
BECOMING AN EXPERT
FISHER OF PEOPLE

The analogy for evangelism of fishing is a good one. I know this because Jesus is the one who made it! When Jesus called his first disciples who were fishermen, he said, "Follow me, and I will make you fishers of men" (Matthew 4:19 ESV). For nearly two millennia, Christians have thought of bringing lost people into the Kingdom of God in terms of fishing.

This sport wasn't really a part of my experience growing up. My knowledge of fishing extended to putting a worm on a hook and casting it into the water, hoping for the best. I don't remember ever catching anything this way. But as a teenager, I did throw a cast net into a canal near my house once and caught a bunch of mullet. I also went deep-sea fishing once hoping to catch sea bass, which was an entirely different experience, and I caught a bunch of fish that day. In that case, the captain knew the exact time and location to go and had the right bait and techniques. Through that limited experience and a little study, I learned there are a lot of different ways to fish. The kind of fish you are trying to catch determines the kind of fishing you do, whether you use certain kinds of fishing line, or bait, or boat, or net, or whatever else. You first determine what kind of fish you want and then fish for them specifically using the best technics for those fish.

For many local churches, their knowledge of fishing for men is the same as what I knew about real fishing. They utilize the "worm on a hook" method, put a sign out in front of the church, and just hope someone comes to faith or joins the church. Or they do one evangelistic program, and when no one "bites," they give up. When someone new joins the leadership team and says, "We should do evangelism," someone whose been around awhile responds, "We tried that already, and it didn't work." Everyone mumbles agreement and then moves on to complain about how the church needs to grow and needs more money but doesn't have a good plan for what to do.

Just as there are many kinds of fish that eat different foods at different depths and at different times, there are different kinds of people with different needs and different resistance levels in coming to Christ. The big idea here is this: first determine who the people around your church are. What are they like? What are their needs? What is their faith like? Once you've learned what kind of people are in your "pond," so to speak, you can more effectively fish for them. Instead of a one-size-fits-all program for evangelism, you can strategize for ways that get them to "nibble" on the gospel while some will actually "bite" and become Christians and join your church! Consider this two-part plan:

Learn about the fish in your pond

Draw a five-mile circle around your church. You've marked out your pond. Analyze the people in your pond. You'll want to discover both demographics – hard data like age and marriage status, incomes, etc., and what's called psychographics – people's felt needs, hopes, and fears, etc. This can be done by general observations, conversations with neighbors, google searches on demographics, or even paid studies that break down a community in detail. If you live in that area, you probably already have a pretty good idea about what your neighbors are like.

Love the fish in your pond

Once you've determined what the people are like, develop a plan that meets needs where they are. Discover how to show them love in practical ways that will cause them to ask you why you are serving them. This can lead to conversations about Jesus' love for them and opportunities to share the Gospel and invite them to church. The American Anglican Council recently conducted a survey that showed that the average age of many Anglican congregations is a concern. It may be scary to see a lack of youth attending your church, but if that's the case for you, no matter how old your congregation may be, if you're still alive, God has a purpose for you. Part of that purpose is to grow His Kingdom and that doesn't depend on age. If you're older, you can love people, pray for people, care for people, and earn the right to share with people. You can do this!

What are the **most significant obstacles** to the **growth of your congregation?**

32% said their **congregation's attitude or actions** were among the most significant obstacles to growth.

15% said the **aging demographics** in their congregation was among the most significant obstacles to growth

11% said the **lack of and inability to reach young families** with children/ youth was among the most significant obstacles to growth

"Inward focus (people unwilling, (not) interested in, lack (of) confidence in reaching outside of the church's walls) average congregation member thinking outreach is the staff's job"

"Congregational members are aging 'Boomers' who are tired, worn-out, and exhausted."

"Busyness among parishioners, Lack of urgency for sharing the Gospel among parishioners"

This is the approach my church took in Jacksonville, Florida. We found that the fish in our pond were mostly lower income people, many of whom were struggling with addictions. Being in the South, most knew something about church and had some knowledge of Jesus. The common belief was, however, that they knew they were sinners and expected judgment from the Church and from God. We learned that no matter how attractive our church was with greeters and signs and excellent worship, our fish just wouldn't come inside our bowl. We had to continually seek ways to connect with them where they were, showing Jesus' love for them in practical ways and earning the right to share the good news with them. Many attempts failed but many also worked amazingly well.

CHAPTER 19:
AVOIDING FUNCTIONAL
UNIVERSALISM

At a worldwide Anglican Conference, GAFCON 2018, which took place in Jerusalem, I attended a breakout seminar led by the Rev. Dr. Kendall Harmon from the United States and the Rev. Rico Tice from the United Kingdom. I chose this seminar for several reasons. Kendall Harmon is one of the leading voices in biblically faithful Anglicanism, I have personally benefitted from Rico Tice's teachings in the Christianity Explored video series, and the topic of the seminar was Hell.

The reality of Hell is a primary motivating factor for me in leading churches through revitalization. Turning a reclining or declining church around is hard. It takes time, and it can be emotionally painful. But the fact that there is Hell for the unrepentant sinner and salvation for the willing makes the hard work, time, and pain worth it. I believe the local church must do whatever it takes to reach those who don't know Jesus and make them His disciples. Maintaining the status quo is not an acceptable option when the possibility exists of one more person going to Hell.

Somewhere in this presentation outlining the various reasons why Hell is often dismissed, even in Biblically faithful churches, the term "Functional Universalism" was used. I was struck by this accurate description of many Anglican churches. Universalists don't lead people to Jesus in order to save them from their sins and their condemnation. They don't believe people need to be saved through Jesus and completely disregard the reality of eternal judgment. If we, as Bible-believing Anglicans, don't lead people to salvation through Jesus because we're too embarrassed to talk about Hell or too afraid to invite someone to repent, then what's the difference? Isn't that just functional Universalism, achieving the same results as those we disagree with?

Anglicans believe that all the Bible is true, even the uncomfortable parts. We believe the scriptures that Jesus is the way, the truth, and the life, and no one comes to the Father except through him (John 14:6). But are unbelievers being saved in our churches? Are we persevering in our mission and bringing unbelievers into a relationship with the Father through Jesus Christ? Or do we just talk about mission and feel good about ourselves for believing the Bible and not being Universalists?

I'm not suggesting that we all start talking about Hell all the time, trying to scare people into Heaven (though I've always said I'd rather be scared into Heaven than stroll blindly into Hell). I am suggesting, however, that if we took the truth that Hell is real more seriously, maybe we'd more willingly push past our fears of evangelism and start doing it.

In the seminar, Rico Tice talked about having to overcome what he called the "pain threshold" of broaching the subject with people. Talking about judgment is scary and produces a lot of fear! But it is still necessary. I remember the first time I prayed with someone who wanted to come to Jesus for salvation. I was physically trembling. But a person's freedom from sin, death, and Hell is more important than my freedom from temporary fear or embarrassment. Love compels courage for their sake.

I wonder what it would look like if every practicing Christian in North America, in view of Hell's reality, loved people enough to overcome their pain threshold and started practicing evangelism. Hearts, congregations, and communities would be transformed. And since Anglicans believe the Bible is true, we can know for sure that we're not alone when doing evangelism. We are partnered with Jesus in his mission. Remember his promise in commissioning us to go: "Behold, I am with you always, to the end of the age" (Matthew 28:20 ESV). He is with you always! May God bless you as you love him more deeply, partner with him more courageously, and go out on mission in the power of the Holy Spirit.

CHAPTER 20:
DOING OUTREACH FOR A CHANGE

As a reminder from previous chapters, the culture around us has radically changed in our lifetime from mostly Christian to largely non-churched. We can't keep doing church the way we've always done it and expect the same results we've always gotten. Every church in the Anglican Church in North America (ACNA) and every true Christian congregation in the Western world, no matter the denomination, must adapt to this change in the culture and adopt a more missional approach if we are going to thrive in the coming years. To be clear, this doesn't mean abandoning your tradition. It is possible to be both Anglican and missional! But if your congregation doesn't adapt to a more missional way of thinking, eventually enough members will move or die that the church will have to close its doors. It is already happening all over North America in every denomination. That doesn't have to be your church's story. Revitalization is possible because all things are possible with God!

In the old model of Christendom, there was often a struggle to be evangelistic because there wasn't a perceived need. Much of the culture was already Christian and society's members were, at least externally, professing members of one Christian church or another. Since congregations were seemingly "doing fine numerically," outreach became something you had to do because Jesus said you had to do it. It might have looked like having an outreach committee that gave some money to a local foodbank or shelter or maybe even sent the occasional volunteer. There was certainly not a lot of zeal behind it, though of course there were zealous individuals here and there. But in many well-established churches, outreach became not much different from a Rotary Club or some other civic organization. Although this practice was not biblical, we got away with this model in the old American culture.

Those days are gone. Now we must do real, purposeful outreach for a change. Our efforts to reach out to the community around our local congregations and meet the physical and emotional needs of others must be done with the ultimate purpose of evangelism. Our goal must be to address people's deeper, spiritual needs and lead them into a saving relationship with Jesus Christ. Once they know about Him, we can help bring them into our church families to make them grow as disciples. There was never a benefit in meeting physical needs while never addressing spiritual needs. Doing so is like holding someone's hand as you walk them straight to Hell. Outreach must be a strategy for being fishers of people.

The Apostle Paul said it best in 1 Corinthians

9:22: "When I am with those who are weak, I share their weakness, for I want to bring the weak to Christ. Yes, I try to find common ground with everyone, doing everything I can to save some" (NLT). The goal of outreach is to show love in a practical way, to develop a relationship with others to find common ground with them, and then point them to Christ for their salvation. Even better is to assimilate them into your church family first to make them disciples.

Although our church didn't know much about recovery, we decided to become experts on it for the sake of those in our communities struggling with addictions. Many came to know Christ and became disciples because of those efforts. After some time, a local outreach ministry called Gleaners joined our church. This ministry gleans food from businesses to give away to those in need. As an outreach ministry, they would serve people in love and lead many to Jesus. Since they weren't a church, they didn't have a means for discipleship and for years they struggled to find a church that would welcome the visibly broken people they were reaching. When they saw our church had a proven track record of welcoming "those people," they were thrilled. Their partnership with us gave our congregation an outreach ministry to call our own which only brought in more people to our spiritual family.

Who are the non-believers, the un-churched, the broken individuals caught in sin in your community? What are their needs? How can your church reach them for a change?

CHAPTER 21:
THE IMPORTANCE OF FUN

Getting visitors does not guarantee that your church will grow, but I guarantee that your church won't grow without getting visitors. I agree with those who argue that the attractional model of church growth is no longer the best model in our largely post-Christian culture, and as I've written already, that we must take on a more missional model where we go out into our surrounding communities to connect with non-believers. Once you connect with them, however, you still have to invite them to a church where, in community, they will be transformed to be like Christ. Inviting people to church remains an essential component of church growth.

Yet, even with all the preaching, teaching, poking, prodding, and sometimes guilting that church members receive about evangelism and invitation, most of the time they don't follow through. In my opinion, reasons for not inviting others to church can be summed up as either immaturity, fear, or selfishness. But even mature, selfless believers, who care deeply about the salvation of those near and far, still don't do much inviting. Fear still grips them. One way to help members with this fear is by creating events that are fun and casual for them to invite people to.

After years of renting worship spaces, our church bought and moved into our own facility and had been used to creating Halloween-alternative events every year as many congregations do. We discovered that a church just down the street had been doing a similar event for 20 years, and it was huge. Despite our own experience doing the same, we decided not to bother competing with them in our new neighborhood. No one in our area was doing any kind of event around Christmas, so we decided to focus on that part of the year. We created a Christmas Carnival with a Chili Cook-off, and, from a purely human standpoint, it was not successful. No one in the church invited anyone else, and attendance was poor. We only had one new attendee who was unchurched, a local mother with her two children who came because of the sign in front of the church offering free chili.

This mother turned out to be an active drug addict who had had bad experiences with church in the past, but she really loved chili. She decided to put up with church people long enough to eat free chili before getting out of there! While at the event, she saw brochures for Celebrate Recovery, the Christ-centered, 12-step ministry our church offered to try to reach the unchurched in our community. While on her second bowl of chili, she commented to a member that she needed recovery and maybe her presence that day wasn't an accident. She was invited to come to church and, of course, Celebrate Recovery. Her first official visit turned out to be a Wednesday night Bible Study. She brought her husband. I taught on Matthew 5:3 that night: "Blessed are the poor in spirit, for theirs is the kingdom of heaven" (NIV). After a small group discussion about this verse, she admitted that being poor in spirit described her. We prayed with her, and she repented and believed in Jesus for salvation and entered God's Kingdom. The following Sunday, her whole family showed up for worship, and her husband became a believer that day. In a short time, they all believed in Jesus and were baptized together as a family, and their lives radically transformed. She began inviting all sorts of people to church, asking them to come and see what Jesus can do. Her changed life led to so many more changed lives, and all that because of some free Christmas chili!

This same woman came to me and suggested maybe the church could do a Sundae Sunday, where we could give away free ice cream sundaes to those in the community. It was a great idea! We discovered the third Sunday of every July is National Ice Cream Day thanks to President Ronald Reagan, so we planned to give everyone a free sundae after the church service. We again encouraged church members to invite unchurched people to come, and this time they did! We had our third largest attendance in Sunday worship in the middle of July! Many new young families visited for the ice cream, but they heard the Gospel proclaimed and had a good experience with church people. New members were added as a result. More lives were transformed. Not all who came joined, but some did! Getting visitors won't guarantee your church will grow, but I guarantee it won't grow without getting visitors.

In the end, one fun event that seemed like a complete failure led to another fun event that was a huge success. What fun event could you create to lower people's defenses and calm their fears when it comes to inviting others? Don't be afraid to try different things. Some will work, some won't, but nothing will work if you don't try.

CHAPTER 22:
THE NEED FOR YOUNG FAMILIES

Have you ever expressed how much your church needs to grow by adding more young families? Have you heard someone else say something like that, particularly in a governing board or vestry meeting? I often hear faithful, older churchgoers say, "We just need to get more young families to come." It is the most common "solution" I hear offered when people start talking about revitalization. For some churches, this really is what is needed, but other churches don't necessarily have to focus on attracting young families; God has something else in mind for them.

Before a church chases after young families, it might be good to first find out if there are even young families within driving distance! There are some areas in Florida, for example, that just don't have that many young families. Churches in those areas are better off focusing on reaching older people, and that's okay! Non-believing, adult human beings are just as much in need of salvation as young people are. They may even be more open to the

Gospel, since they may be more aware of the certainty of death and judgment!

Rather than starting with knee-jerk solutions and assuming more young families is the final answer, it's better to ask, "Who is God specifically calling our church to reach with the Good News in our community?" God is probably not calling you to reach all the different groups of people in your neighborhood. He will reach them through different churches, each doing their part. God's answer for your church might in fact be young families, but even then, you'll want to ask, "What are the young families in our community like?" Not all young families are the same. What are their physical and spiritual needs? How can you serve and relationally connect with the specific unchurched young families around your church? Hoping that there are already young Christian families in your area that could choose your church will not work anymore. If that's your plan, you'll probably be disappointed. Hope is not a strategy.

God's answer to you might be to reach the older generations; maybe empty nesters, or maybe people addicted to opioids or other addicts, or maybe veterans, or maybe single moms, or maybe whoever else is near your church that doesn't know Jesus. Whoever God calls you to reach, you'll want to understand how to serve and connect with them in order to save some.

As mentioned in a previous chapter, the Apostle Paul describes his own attitude regarding his mission in 1 Corinthians 9:20-22:

"When I was with the Jews, I lived like a Jew to

bring the Jews to Christ. When I was with those who follow the Jewish law, I too lived under that law. Even though I am not subject to the law, I did this so I could bring to Christ those who are under the law. When I am with the Gentiles who do not follow the Jewish law, I too live apart from that law so I can bring them to Christ. But I do not ignore the law of God; I obey the law of Christ. When I am with those who are weak, I share their weakness, for I want to bring the weak to Christ. Yes, I try to find common ground with everyone, doing everything I can to save some." (NLT)

Who is the group of people you're called to "find common ground with?"

Again, thinking about this using Jesus' analogy of being "fishers of men" (Matt. 4:19) is helpful. Think of the community around your church as your "fishing pond." Who are the "fish" in your pond? Once you identify the fish in your pond that you want to catch, you can plan accordingly. If you want to catch bass (young families) and there are no bass (young families) in your pond, you'll fish all day long without success. If you're throwing out bait meant for bass but there are only trout (empty nesters), for example, the trout (empty nesters) won't be interested. If you identify the trout and use the bait they like, there's a higher chance some will be interested. I think you get the idea. If you search for ways to attract young families but there are no young families in your area, you'll be wasting a lot of energy for little results.

PART 1 DISCUSSION QUESTIONS
VISION FOR EVANGELISM AND MISSION

1. Canon Mark described the possibility of being essentially Functional Universalists. Do you agree or disagree with this possibly being a problem and why?
2. He described the "Pain Threshold" that needs to be overcome to do evangelism. What are some pain thresholds, or fears, that you will have to overcome to practice evangelism?
3. Does the analogy of the being "fishers of people" make sense to you for your and your congregation's practice of evangelism and mission? Why or why not?
4. Who are the unchurched living around your congregation? What are their needs, and how can your church meet those needs in a practical way?
5. Based on your answers to question 4, what are some ways your church can do outreach to them for a change?

6. What fun event could you create to lower people's defenses and calm their fears when it comes to inviting others? (e.g. the Sundae Sunday that Canon Mark used as an example)

7. To drive this essential point home again, who is God specifically calling your church to reach with the Gospel in your community? What are some ways you could go about reaching that group?

PART 2:

INTENTIONAL WORSHIP

CHAPTER 23:
SEEKER INSENSITIVE CHURCHES

I once heard that the number one emotion people feel when going to church for the first time is fear. They ask themselves: Will I fit in? What will be expected of me? Am I dressed right? There are a lot of unknowns that can cause fear.

Not too long ago, I experienced this firsthand. Becoming the full-time Director for Church Revitalization and Coaching for the American Anglican Council (AAC), I found myself in the interesting situation of having to find a church home now that I would no longer be a pastor of a local church. For nearly two decades, I went to church where I worked. I may have visited other churches on occasion, but that was more as a spy to gather good ideas than as a casual visitor hoping for a spiritual home. Visiting a congregation to see if it was a safe place for my family was different. I felt fearful.

I visited two churches. I was friends with both pastors and was recognized by parishioners when I walked in. I knew the cultures of each place, so I knew how to dress. With all that in place, I still felt fearful. Would I like it? Would my family like it? I hope they don't make me put on a nametag (thankfully, neither church did). If I, a seasoned church attendee and minister felt fearful, how much more would a non-believer walking in feel fearful? Being sensitive to that fear in our visitors is not only loving but vital to successful church health and growth.

You might be familiar with the concept of being "seeker sensitive" or "seeker friendly." Many Anglicans I know have an automatic negative reaction to the concept and feel that even if I just use that term, I'm suggesting abandoning scripture, liturgy, and tradition for a new tradition of fog machines, light shows, skinny jeans, and consumerism. However, when I use the term, I'm not suggesting any of that. What I am suggesting is that at times our traditions can cause us to become seeking insensitive, and there is a happy median that churches can walk.

One definition of the word insensitive is to be "deficient in consideration." Deficient is defined as "lacking something," so to be seeker insensitive would mean to be lacking in consideration for those who visit our church. There are ways to consider the needs of visitors without sacrificing truth and liturgical integrity. Often, we have our worship services primarily for those already in Church and with little to no consideration or sensitivity for what visitors would experience when they come in. If you find the term "seeker sensitive" unnerving to you given its association with some consumerism driven mega churches, let me instead simply use the word kind. In the end, considering the needs of others coming into the church is a kind thing to do. Being kind and hospitable to visitors doesn't have to lead to watering down anything. It should lead to greater love expressed through concrete action toward your neighbor.

Kindness to strangers and visitors among God's people is not a modern church issue. It's a Biblical issue that was spoken about all the way back in the Old Testament. And in Luke 6, where Jesus taught on loving one's enemies saying, "Do to others as you would have them do to you," concludes, "But love your enemies, do good to them, and lend to them without expecting to get anything back. Then your reward will be great, and you will be children of the Most High, because he is kind to the ungrateful and wicked. Be merciful, just as your Father is merciful" (NIV). More often than not, visitors to our churches will not even be enemies! If we're commanded to be kind to our enemies, how much more should we be kind, considerate, and merciful to our visitors.

If you have objections to the modern, seeker sensitive concept but don't want to be seeker insensitive, there are solid, useful ways to gear your congregation to be kind towards visitors whether they are "seekers" or not:

1. Have greeters and friendly ushers welcoming people in every week. In addition, have every member see themselves as a greeter on Sunday mornings with everyone looking out for visitors and being willing to break from their conversations with those they know to at least say hello to newcomers. Many churches are small enough to recognize new faces. In larger churches, visitors

can by spotted by looking out for those walking slower than everyone else and reading the signage to get around!

2. At the beginning of worship, take a moment to welcome those visiting that day. Assume newcomers are not familiar with either the liturgy/service or other aspects of the community and explain as needed how it all works. I made it a habit of doing this every week, even if I knew there were no visitors because I wanted the members to know that if they invited someone they could be confident that Fr. Mark would make sure they would be welcomed knowing that I did it every time.

3. Put your bulletins together with visitors in mind. What will they read? Will it make sense to them? Is it clear when to stand up, sit down, kneel? Is there a coffee hour? During the age of Christendom, we could assume most visitors probably knew the Sunday morning basics, but now we should never assume that. Present your materials with the unchurched in mind and seasoned church visitors will be fine, too.

CHAPTER 24:
FIRST IMPRESSIONS MATTER

I once walked my church's property with an owner of a landscaping business trying to get a bid on the cost of cutting the grass. I was busy, as usual, and just wanted the bottom-line cost from him. I got much more. He pointed out how trees and bushes could look better and suggested adding fresh flowers by the front door, and on and on it went. I grew impatient. But then he talked about how important first impressions are, how people can judge places by their appearance. He gave an example of moving to a new town and looking for a neighborhood to live in, and people often make snap judgments based on the exteriors of properties and streets. People make instant decisions on whether a neighborhood is "thriving" or "declining" and whether they'd want to live there by a first impression. In that moment, his statement was an epiphany for me. It just made sense. For better or worse, people make quick and lasting judgments on places like neighborhoods, restaurants, and hotels based on first impressions. They do it for people, too. Why wouldn't they do the same for churches? Of course, they do.

What are people's first impressions of your church? When we take the "V" in the vitals of church health seriously and go out from the church, build relationships with unbelievers, and get up the nerve to invite them, what will their experience be if they come? Landscaping is a very small part of it. Other factors can be much more important: signage, parking lot setup, cobwebs and cleanliness, handicap access, children's ministry, a warm welcome or not, and more! All these things are what visitors will notice even before the service starts. You can have the best music, sermon, or liturgical aesthetics, but if a person's first impression is a bad one before they even get into the service, it will be that much harder to overcome and get them to come back. On the other hand, if they have a good first impression from the car to the service, they will be able to make a decision on returning for a second visit based on the more important things like the liturgy, preaching, music, and people. Though we can't cater to everyone's perceptions, it is essential to think through and care about our visitors' first impressions as best as we are able.

I attended a clergy conference during which I mentioned to a group of clergy that I was going to become a new rector. One of them turned to me and said I should write down everything I see that needs to be changed in the first thirty days. After thirty days, he said, I'd become part of the institution and wouldn't be able to notice those things anymore. He was so right. I took his advice and came up with a two-page list of things I saw that needed to be addressed. Then, over the next three years, we fixed them all! For most of us who have been in our church for a while, we stop seeing what new people see. We are part of the institution. Our eyes pass over the issues that visitors see.

Let me suggest a few ideas to get started on making good first impressions:

1. Realize that first impressions matter and commit to making improvements for visitors a priority.

2. Try to view your church through a visitor's eyes. You can do this by pretending to be a visitor in your church for the first time. As you drive up and park, as you walk toward the entrance, as you enter the service, would you feel welcomed and know where to go? Write down what you see that needs to be addressed.

3. Make a plan to address these issues over time. Small things can be addressed quickly. Bigger problems take time.

4. In all things, remember what God's word says, "Be wise in the way you act toward outsiders; make the most of every opportunity" (Colossians 4:5 NIV).

CHAPTER 25:
TEN STEPS TOWARD HOSPITALITY

Have you realized how we tend to notice things in our home when guests are coming that we might otherwise overlook? The dust on the bookshelf, or the dirt on the baseboards, or the junk mail on the counter are all fine when it's just "us," but when guests are coming, they move up on our priority list! Guests have a way of motivating us to present our best. It often comes from a desire to be hospitable and create a pleasant atmosphere. Hospitality is defined on Dictionary.com as "the quality of receiving and treating guests and strangers in a warm, friendly, generous way." It's generous to give guests our best.

Hospitality is built into our Christian ethics and our worldview. When Jesus taught on the Final Judgement, he described the King inviting the righteous into the Kingdom in part due to their hospitality. Their response tells us about this hospitality: "Then these righteous ones will reply, 'Lord, when did we ever see you hungry and feed you? Or thirsty and give you something to drink? Or a stranger and show you hospitality? Or naked and give you clothing? When did we ever see you sick or in prison and visit you?' And the King will say, 'I tell you the truth, when you did it to one of the least of these my brothers and sisters, you were doing it to me!'" (Matthew 25:37-40). Making guests feel comfortable may not be in the same vein as feeding those who are starving, but it shows the same motivation: to meet a need. Humans want to feel loved and welcome. Receiving guests and strangers in a warm, friendly, and generous way is an important aspect of living out our faith in Jesus.

Just as we get comfortable in our own homes and overlook things when guests aren't coming, in our "church homes" we can also get too comfortable and fail to notice things that need change. In so doing, we might be less than hospitable. Without having regular visitors to our churches, we can get lulled into a mentality that says, "It's just going to be us again today, so why does it really matter?" Instead, to be healthy and grow we should assume guests are coming to our churches every Sunday and act as if that's the case whether they do or not. If you do this, you'll pay closer attention to details, and your confidence in your church's ability to receive guests will create greater inspiration for more invitation.

Here are ten steps you can take toward making your church more hospitable every week whether guests come or not:

1. **Be Clean.** Keep the church clean like you would your own house when you're having guests over. If a guest came, would you leave that clutter there or

that smudge over there? Be faithful in the little things.

2. **Be Warm and Friendly.** Install greeters and ushers and go out among the people yourself if you are the pastor. Make sure everyone is greeted with a smile when they come in. A smile and a handshake can go a long way.

3. **Be Party Ready.** I was once told being "party ready" meant being ready ten minutes before guests arrive. That way you're not scrambling around with last minute details instead of focusing on them when they get there. As the lead pastor, I always tried to have my sermon prep done and issues with the service and the ministry team addressed by at least ten minutes before the service, so I could warmly welcome people as they arrived, both members and guests.

4. **Be Excellent.** Strive for excellence in every aspect of Sunday Worship - before, during, and after the service(s). Not perfection, but excellence. It honors the Lord by providing our best to him and to our guests.

5. **Have Good Coffee Available.** Not only do people like coffee, but guests often feel social anxiety at a new place. Letting people get a cup of coffee gives them something to do and having a cup in their hands can create a comforting barrier for them. Also, if they have a hot cup of coffee after the service, they are more likely to stick around longer, and you will have a chance to talk and build relationships with them!

6. **Release People with the Gift of Hospitality.** Hospitality is like evangelism in that we're all called to do it, but some are just more naturally gifted at it than others. Find hospitality-gifted people in your congregation and put them in charge of more.

7. **Have a Welcome Center.** Create some space where guests can find information about your church. Make it visible and accessible. Anticipate questions your guests will have and create quality handouts with answers. Having a handout gives them something to do by reading it. If they linger after church and are looking at information, they send the message that they are interested. It doesn't guarantee they'll come back, but it's more likely than the ones who leave immediately!

8. **Have Clear Signage Inside and Out.** It's generous to your guests to make it clear where everything is. We had a sign by the women's bathroom but were constantly asked where the bathroom was. It seemed so obvious to us, and plus there was a sign! We finally realized that when people exited the sanctuary, the sign couldn't be seen in its current position. We moved the sign to the other side of the bathroom door, and it solved the problem.

9. **Lead the Service.** Lead the liturgy/service with guests in mind. Don't assume they are already Anglican or are familiar with your kind of church service. Then lead in a way that is "warm, friendly, and generous". There are simple ways of doing this

that flow well and won't detract from a focus on God.

10. **Give a Gift.** This is fairly standard now, but it's still a good idea to keep in mind. Have a gift for newcomers at the Welcome Center. Also, if you get their mailing address, you can send them a gift in the mail the week of their visit. Be creative. We once had good results by simply mailing some $5.00 Walmart gift cards to newcomers as a thank you for coming because it was different. Be creative. What would be generous and make your church memorable to them?

CHAPTER 26:
ACCEPTANCE VERSUS APPROVAL

I once wrote a series of articles about the letters to the seven churches found in in the Book of Revelation. My focus was church revitalization, looking to see what those churches were said to have needed and how we could apply that to our Anglican churches. In the letter to the Church in Pergamum, the focus was on how the church there needed the approval of human beings. In my articles, I titled the section on this church, "The Compromising Church," which seems appropriate given the word of God to them:

"Write this letter to the angel of the church in Pergamum. This is the message from the one with the sharp two-edged sword: 'I know that you live in the city where Satan has his throne, yet you have remained loyal to me. You refused to deny me even when Antipas, my faithful witness, was martyred among you there in Satan's city. But I have a few complaints against you. You tolerate some among you whose teaching is like that of Balaam, who showed Balak how to trip up the people of Israel. He taught them to sin by eating food offered to idols and by committing sexual sin. In a similar way, you have some Nicolaitans among you who follow the same teaching. Repent of your sin, or I will come to you suddenly and fight against them with the sword of my mouth. Anyone with ears to hear must listen to the Spirit and understand what he is saying to the churches. To everyone who is victorious I will give some of the manna that has been hidden away in heaven. And I will give to each one a white stone, and on the stone will be engraved a new name that no one understands except the one who receives it." Revelation 2:12-17 (NLT)

Pergamum was a center for "Caesar Worship" in that part of the Roman Empire. The Christians there were commended for not bowing to "Caesar as Lord" but acknowledging "Jesus Christ as Lord," even in the face of martyrdom. Despite this positive quality, they were still apparently compromising theologically and morally with some aspects of the culture. Though the civic leaders of Pergamum had the power of the sword to kill them, the Christians were encouraged to remember that Jesus' sword was mightier and that he deserved their uncompromised obedience.

In thinking about how this might apply to churches today, an interesting idea came to me. Many Anglican churches came out of the theologically and morally compromised Episcopal Church, and they are still careful not to compromise with the culture. They were burned once and don't want it to ever happen again. For these churches, this was a costly lesson to learn, both in terms of spiritual pain and physical loss, especially buildings. Protecting the truth and integrity of our witness to Christ's saving power and lordship is essential. I do wonder if some of those churches harm their witness by figuratively building up too many walls around themselves to fortify that separation from corrupting influences. I wonder if our fear of being compromised again hinders our effectiveness at bringing the Gospel of the Kingdom to our local communities. It's a line that's often hard to walk and a struggle I'm sure was familiar to the Church in Pergamum and should be familiar to us, especially amid our own cultural conflicts.

The Gospel of the Kingdom of Heaven should engage and penetrate the culture wherever possible. Christianity is not a religion that says, "We good people are in, and we need to keep those bad people out." The Church is a hospital for the sick. Local churches are meant to be missional outposts and not walled-up compounds. I have even witnessed church leadership that avoided bringing in unchurched people because they thought it could lead to compromise with the culture. In his book, Richard Niebuhr addressed this problem. Christ and Culture is a standard read for most seminarians and speaks to the challenge of how to be in the world but not of the world and how that's been a struggle for centuries. We must wrestle with it today if we are to survive and thrive.

If your local church is going to revitalize and grow, it cannot develop a protectionist, Christ-against-culture attitude, while at the same time, it must adhere to the Truth it first received as the Church of Christ. It must missionally engage with unbelievers and sinners in the community, bringing them to Christ and into his body to be transformed as we've discussed much in this book, all the while avoiding being affected in a negative way by their struggles and their sins.

So, how can we be welcoming to everyone without becoming a theologically and morally compromised church? A simple answer is coming to grips with and adopting the principle of acceptance versus approval. We accept all people. We do not approve of all beliefs and behaviors.

At a former congregation I led not long after leaving the Episcopal church, we negotiated a lease for rented space. One of our members invited the new landlord to come to our church. She came and brought her brother who was openly homosexual and whose lifestyle conflicted with what the Bible teaches about human sexuality. Within weeks of their attendance, this man was diagnosed with stage four cancer and was admitted into the hospital. I visited him when I heard. Almost right away, he asked me, "You know I'm gay, right? I really like coming to your church. I want to keep attending. Would it be okay since I'm gay?" The answer might be easy to say because Christians have often heard it: "We love the sinner but hate the sin." Of course, it would be okay. But having fought for a decade against the Episcopal Church's false teachings on human sexuality, I knew at that moment that I had to give myself a "gut check." Did I really love him despite his views and his sin which I had fought so hard against in my former denomination?

It turns out I really did. I told him that though he was gay, he was of course welcome to come any time. I added that he needed to know, in a spirit of full disclosure, that as a Christian church we believed that all sex outside of marriage between one man and one woman was sin; he'd hear that from the pulpit. Whenever I preached on that subject, he could be sure I wasn't just singling him out or even a group of people but all who needed freedom from sin, whether an adulterer or homosexual or cohabitating couples. The man nodded gently and said he thought that's what we believed, he understood it, and it was fine with him. He still wanted to come. He heard that he was accepted as a human being made in God's image, even though his lifestyle wasn't approved of. He continued to attend, but within months was in hospice care. His sister called me one day saying that he was near death. She asked if I could come pray with him. I shared the gospel with him and his partner, who was also there listening intently and nodding in agreement to everything I said. The man's partner encouraged him to accept Jesus as his Savior and Lord, and I prayed with him to do just that, and he was saved. The deacon who was with me got a bowl of water from the kitchen, and we baptized him right there on his literal death bed. He died soon after.

God wanted that man with him for all eternity. Since we were willing to accept him as a person loved by God without compromising about his behavior, we participated in God's saving work. Not only that, from that conversion many more people heard about it and ended up coming to the church and being transformed as well.

PART 2 DISCUSSION QUESTIONS
INTENTIONAL WORSHIP

1. Reflect on the worship service at your church. How considerate is it to visitors? Would you say that a visitor would be welcome, and it would be easy for them to participate, or not, and why?
2. How could your church be more intentionally kind to visitors before during and after the worship service(s)?
3. What are some ways your church could improve the first impressions a visitor would have when they came to your worship service from the time they pulled onto the property to the beginning of the worship service?
4. Go back and review the ten steps suggested to be hospitable to guests in chapter 25. How is your church doing at applying those steps? Can you think of other ways your church could be more hospitable to visitors? If so, please describe.

5. How can your church protect against being too protective? How can your church practice engaging with a corrupt culture without compromising the faith? How can you accept sinful people without approving of sinful behavior?

PART 3:
TRANSFORMATION TO CHRISTLIKENESS

CHAPTER 27:
TRANSFORMATION TO
CHRISTLIKENESS

In a survey of Anglican Church in North America clergy conducted by the American Anglican Council, 32% cited their congregation's attitude or actions as being among the most significant obstacles to growth. That is not surprising. At a national conference on church revitalization, the speakers said one of the biggest barriers to church growth in all churches is the resistant attitudes in the minds of the church members. They referred to this as an immaturity problem. One speaker called it "the perpetual adolescence of the Church."

This isn't a new phenomenon. We can read a lot about immaturity in the Church in the Bible. The Apostle Paul writing to the Church in Corinth wrote, "I gave you milk, not solid food, for you were not yet ready for it. Indeed, you are still not ready" (1 Cor. 3:2 NIV). And again, "Brothers and sisters, stop thinking like children. In regard to evil be infants, but in your thinking be adults" (1 Cor. 14:20 NIV). In other words, "Grow up!"

If immaturity is a common barrier to growth in the Church, what is the solution? The leaders in the congregation must strive to raise the maturity level of the church's members. In order to do that, a spiritual growth plan for them becomes very important. This type of plan moves people from immaturity to maturity, from selfishness to selflessness, from being self-centered to Christ-centered, from being consumers to contributors. Simply hoping people will grow up on their own won't work. Sunday sermons alone won't work. Even getting people into small group Bible studies or Sunday School classes won't necessarily work. There are plenty of Christians who go to church and Bible study every week who are still selfish, continue in their sins without spiritual transformation, and resist the mission to reach the lost.

Here's the point, every local church needs a clear plan for how to move members through the process of transformation. Jesus was the perfect human being. He still is, though now he's glorified. When He walked the earth, He lived his human life for the sake of others. He continues to give us that life now. Each church needs a discipleship path that ends with the goal of members living out their faith in the same way – becoming Christlike in every way. As Paul wrote in Philippians 2:4-8, "Don't look out only for your own interests, but take an interest in others, too. You must have the same attitude that Christ Jesus had. Though he was God, he did not think of equality with God as something to cling to. Instead, he gave up his divine privilege; he took the humble position of a slave and was born as a human being. When he appeared in human form, he humbled himself in obedience to God and died a criminal's death on a cross." (NLT)

What is your church's plan for making mature, obedient followers of Jesus Christ who are transformed into his likeness? Is there a plan, and is it clear, clearly communicated, and doable? If not, pray about how to engage in Christian discipleship in your context, commit to a plan, and implement it throughout next year.

CHAPTER 28:
RAISING THE MATURITY LEVEL
IN YOUR CHURCH

As part of my preparation for the priesthood, I was required to meet with various priests before and during seminary to ask questions and have them pass on wisdom. One of my biggest surprises in those times was the consistent theme about the ongoing struggle clergy had to disciple people. No one I talked to had a clear plan that worked. I remember thinking, "How come no one seems to have figured this out after almost 2000 years of Christianity?"

I started sketching out plans and processes that I could implement when I became a local church leader. About that same time, I was assigned the book, The Purpose Driven Church, by Rick Warren in one of my classes. When I finally read the book, I realized I didn't need to reinvent the wheel and could adapt some of his ideas to an Anglican local church context. I saw many lives transformed to Christian maturity by moving people through a series of classes like what he developed for his church. Now, over 20 years later, I have learned there are a lot of different plans for discipleship out there that are effective. It doesn't matter which plan a local church uses as much as whether there is actually a plan in place!

Most churches I've consulted with for revitalization have no well-thought-out plan to make disciples who are transformed into Christlikeness and who then reach out to those around them. Not having a discipleship strategy causes a church to be out of balance in the church vitals and, therefore, unhealthy. This contributes to the lack of growth and/or decline.

If your church is in that situation, let me encourage you to prayerfully develop a discipleship plan that suits your context. Here are some principles that you can include in your plan to help raise your church's level of maturity:

Spiritual Growth Is Intentional

This was something I didn't understand for quite a while. Having grown up in the church but never really knowing Christ as my Lord, I decided in my early 20s that I was done with church. It was only after leaving the church that I got saved! This happened while sitting on a couch, by myself, watching a Christian VHS tape (some of you will remember VHS tapes) on Intelligent Design. Of course, encountering Truth, receiving Jesus, and being born again outside of a local church context left me without any real guidance from God's people. I had to start figuring it out on my own, and I did it with the leading of the Holy Spirit. I assumed that spiritual growth was like that for everyone: pray the prayer of salvation, follow the Holy Spirit's leading, and that's all we need. As I led people to the Lord myself, I found I would often move on to the next person thinking they would automatically grow from there and be okay. My job was over, God could take it from there! However, often those people who were born again remained "babies" and weren't maturing on their own. Over time, I realized my experience was more of an exception than a norm.

Spiritual growth is not automatic. There are many obstacles to our faith, not the least are the world, the flesh, and the devil. New believers need a clear pathway to move them towards Christ in a deeper way. They need the support and protection of a community. They need a discipleship plan walked out with others to lead them to living like Christ. As leaders, we need to be intentional about building people up in the communities we lead knowing it won't just happen automatically.

Spiritual Growth is Incremental

Growth doesn't happen instantly. One of the most important aspects of any plan is that it allows people to grow over time. Wouldn't it be great if we all came out of baptismal waters instantly changed and perfect like Christ? It would be so much easier! But that doesn't happen. After the Red Sea, there's the wilderness. We learn to walk and grow incrementally. Babies are the same. They start out needing their parents' care and provision and only later begin sharing the family's responsibility. When they mature, they go out and multiply the life they received from their parents. New believers are "babies" in Christ, so whatever plan you implement in your church, it needs to be a step by step process that keeps this reality in mind. The Bible says, "So all of us who have had that veil removed can see and reflect the glory of the Lord. And the Lord—who is the Spirit—makes us more and more like him as we are changed into his glorious image" (2 Corinthians 3:18 NLT).

Spiritual Growth is Incarnational

No matter how good our discipleship plan, it will only be effective if the Lord is at work in the person's heart. This is why there are so many church members who have plenty of head knowledge about the Bible or the Church, but their lives haven't been transformed to Christlikeness. Maturity is more about the work of God in our hearts by the Holy Spirit than it is about simply imitating others. It is true that a person needs to intentionally work towards growth and learn to make good choices that lead to their maturity, just as babies do, but they must do so recognizing it is God who provides the power to transform their hearts. It says in Philippians 2:12b-13 that the Christians should "continue to work out your salvation with fear and trembling, for it is God who works in you to will and to act in order to fulfill his good purpose" (NIV). You work out, and God works in! True life transformation, like church transformation, is a partnership between you and God through the Holy Spirit.

CHAPTER 29:
THREE-FOLD MATURITY

In the last chapter, I wrote about the need for every local church to have a plan for discipleship. If the goal is to see people go from being lost and cut off from God in their sin to mature Christians on mission to others, the Church must have a way to move them through that process. Although it would be nice if there was one, sure-fire plan that every local church in every community could apply, this is not the case. Spiritual growth plans must be formed and tweaked to fit the specific people you're trying to help grow. For example, the exact plan that worked for Pastor Rick Warren in a Southern California suburban culture that I read about in seminary wasn't what worked exactly for my church in a lower income depressed part of my city in North Florida. However, the principles were the same and could be adapted to fit different contexts and Christian traditions. Here are three wise principles found in every discipleship plan that effectively help people be transformed that you can incorporate into your congregation's plan. These three make maturity a three-fold concept that is the destiny of every person in Christ:

Spiritual Growth is Scriptural

At the time I originally wrote the article that became this chapter, it was around the 500th anniversary of the Protestant Reformation. The Reformation's emphasis on the Word of God and its accessibility to all people was critical to the revitalization of the Church, and the Word is just as critical today in the individual's heart as much as it is for the sake of the whole church. I remember hearing a professor in seminary talk about preaching. He made a dismissive comment about not having every sermon's application be to read the Bible more. Although I understood what he was trying to get at, I remember thinking, "Why not make that application every time?" It may not be the only thing we need to do, but it's a foundational thing to do and most Christians I know think they should read and study it more.

So, over the years I have found myself adding that encouragement somewhere in my sermons almost weekly. I likened it to the classic joke about the new priest who, on his first Sunday, preached a good sermon. Everyone complimented it. The next Sunday he preached the exact same sermon. Everyone figured it was just a fluke and didn't say anything. The third Sunday, he preached the same exact sermon again! Finally, someone asked him if he knew he preached the same sermon three weeks in a row. He replied, "Yes, and when you get that one down, I'll move on to the next one!" No matter how often I challenged people to regularly read the Bible on their own in order to deepen their relationship with God, most people struggled to make it a habit. They needed the reminders. Whatever your church's spiritual growth plan is, it must include teaching on how and why to "read, mark, learn, and inwardly digest" the Scriptures in order to apply them for the purpose of spiritual transformation.

Spiritual Growth is Relational

We only grow in community. One of the marks of Christlikeness is producing the Fruit of the Spirit described in Galatians 5:22, "love, joy, peace, patience, kindness, goodness, faithfulness, gentleness, and self-control" (NIV). You can think you are super-loving while alone at home reading the Bible, but it's only when you're around unlovable people that you find out if you really love well! The same is true of the other fruit in that list. Patience is a classic one. You can be confident you've grown in patience until you pick the wrong line at the grocery store. In community, we see our limitations and put into practice our transformation. This is one of the main reasons God has called us into community.

Small groups are a very effective tool to help foster this relational aspect of discipleship. God often puts EGR ("Extra Grace Required") people in every group to help us grow. Some people just irritate us, for whatever reason, and you most likely irritate other people! These kinds of people help us see our shortcomings and push us to greater love. Some other relational tools are retreats, mentors, and ministry teams. We read in Hebrews 10:24-25: "Let us think of ways to motivate one another to acts of love and good works. And let us not neglect our meeting together, as some people do, but encourage one another, especially now that the day of his return is drawing near" (NLT).

Spiritual Growth is Experiential

So often, we limit our discipleship to just attending classes. Things like Sunday school, Bible studies, and sermons are all that is expected to move people to maturity. These are great things. People have to acquire godly knowledge and wisdom somehow. But if that is the extent of their growth process, it can lead to a lot of "head" knowledge without a lot of application or internal change. As we apply what we know with the help of others, our knowledge becomes experiential. The spiritual information finally "clicks" and gets into our heart, becoming spiritual action.

Early on in my ministry, I was trying to move my congregation to be more missional in our local community. I was preaching about it and teaching classes on it, but it was when we did a 40-Day Campaign on missions that it really took root in our church. During the campaign, the whole church was focused on that one topic for six weeks. Everyone was in a small group, and each small group participated in a major missional outreach project in our local community. I was amazed to watch the members experience the joy of putting others' needs ahead of their own. After that campaign, there was no turning back. The church had a taste for mission in the community, and it got into the DNA of the church. More spiritual growth took place in six weeks of experiencing Christlikeness than a year's worth of sermons and classes could do. The relational component was also at work. I watched all sorts of conflicts pop up, and people learned how to quickly forgive and make amends because they had to get back to the projects at hand. The mission became too important to let conflicts derail it.

CHAPTER 30:
PREACHING FOR A CHANGE

There's a difference in preaching and teaching. Certainly, preaching contains teaching, however preaching is something more – at least it should be. The goal of preaching is the transformation of lives. I once heard someone say that "preaching goes for the guts." I liked that and often have that in the back of my mind when preparing sermons. Please don't be offended if you are a teacher. Teaching is essential and as I just wrote, preaching must contain teaching. It's just that preaching takes good teaching and adds to it the "so what" that will turn the transfer of information into life transformation.

Transforming people into Christlikeness is what preachers preach for, right? It's not about impressing people with our speaking ability or intelligence. It's not just about passing on head knowledge about the Bible. It's about transforming lives for Jesus Christ. Right? Pews full of people who just know all about Jesus won't be the missional disciples that North America desperately needs in our times. We need pews full of people who intimately know Jesus and are daily being transformed into his likeness – people who are living as Jesus would in the world around them. In our pulpits we must be preaching for a change: a change of life. A change from selfish consumers into mature missional selfless contributors for God's Kingdom in the world.

For those of you reading this who are in the Anglican Church of North America, do you remember what its mission statement is? Here it is, "Reaching North America With Teaching About Jesus Christ." Wait, no. That's not it. It is actually, "Reaching North America with the Transforming love of Jesus Christ." Our mission as Anglicans in North America is to reach every human being in North America so that their lives are changed through a personal, growing relationship with Jesus. If you are a preacher, are you preaching for a change? Here are four ways to do just that:

1. **Give Regular Invitations to Believe in Christ for Salvation.** I can guarantee you that a person won't be changed into mature Christlikeness if they aren't even born again in the first place. I was in church for years giving the outward appearance of being a Christ follower, however it wasn't until I prayed a prayer to believe in Jesus, his death and resurrection for the forgiveness of my sins, and had the Holy Spirit dwelling within me that I began to be transformed. The Holy Spirit no doubt is drawing people to the Father prior to their salvation, however true transformation of life from the inside out won't happen if they are not even a

believer. You don't have to force an invitation into every sermon however more often than not it naturally fits to say, "If you're here today and you've never prayed this prayer, please pray along with me…" If you want to see lives changed, help people take that first step and not just hope they do sometime after the sermon.

2. **Give people the "So What."** So what are they supposed to do with the information in the message? A sermon is not a Bible Study, so when you teach about the original Greek of some word that's super informing – so what are they to do to apply that into their life that week? Preaching for a change is adding to good Biblical teaching the "So What" applications. I adopted an Application based approach to preaching where my main points (derived from the Biblical text) would be the applications so they were easy to remember. Even if you feel strongly about preaching classic expository sermons, you can still place strong emphasis on the applications throughout the sermon. Too often so much really good Biblical information is proclaimed and then due to a shortage of time, a couple quick applications are thrown in at the end – almost like an afterthought. Try adding more emphasis on the applications to your messages with a, "Would you this week…." adding whatever applications the text and the Lord is challenging them with. Also, I recommend preaching more "How To" messages instead of "Ought To" messages. Many believers already

know what they ought to do. It's the how to application that they often need help with.

3. **Give Hand-Outs or a "Sermon Notes" section in the bulletin.** Many people absorb information better when their hands are writing. I'm an auditory learner so I'm good with just listening, but I've found so many people appreciated being able to write down their "take-aways" from the message as they heard them. Later, they could also refer to their notes during the week. I assumed that most people would forget most of what I said by the time they got to the parking lot (sadly considering how much work goes into sermons), however by given them opportunities to write applications down it gives them a better chance to retain what they heard and see their lives changed for the good. Small groups could even use these notes for a mid-week study to go deeper into the points made in the message.

4. **Give People The Opportunity to Make Commitments.** Good ideas don't transform lives. Commitments do. Like, believing it's a good idea to have a daily quiet time to know God and read the Word but never doing it won't change your life. However, making a commitment to a daily quiet time and doing it faithfully over time, will absolutely bring change to your life. Rather than letting people just smile and nod at the good idea you are challenging them with, ask people to make a commitment that day to put into practice whatever the application is that day or week. Some

examples are, would you commit to Christ as your savior and Lord? or would you commit to tithing? or would you commit to joining a small group? or whatever? People are what they are committed to. Don't be afraid to preach for a change and ask people to make commitments.

PART 3 DISCUSSION QUESTIONS
TRANSFORMATION TO CHRISTLIKENESS

1. Think about how you have been discipled to be transformed into Christlikeness since you've been a Christian. What was most helpful? What didn't work?

2. Do you think the way you were discipled prepared you to be missional and share Jesus with others? If not, given the changes in our culture, do you agree or disagree that your church needs a plan to mature people in such a way that includes being missional and why?

3. What is your church's plan for making mature, obedient followers of Jesus Christ who are transformed into his likeness? If there is a plan, is it clear, clearly communicated, and doable? If so, please describe it. If your church does not have a discipleship plan, would you pray about how to engage Christian discipleship in your context, commit to a plan, and implement it throughout

next year? The next two questions are designed to help you think about what to put into that plan:

4. Canon Mark described that there is no one right plan to make disciples, however, good discipleship plans are intentional, incremental, and incarnational (see chapter 29). How could you incorporate these elements into your discipleship pathway?

5. Three other ingredients that should be "baked in" to any good discipleship plan are that they are Scriptural, relational, and experiential (see chapter 30). How could you incorporate these elements into your plan?

PART 4:

AUTHENTIC COMMUNITY

CHAPTER 31:
LOVING YOUR
DYSFUNCTIONAL FAMILY

I went to Disney World the day after Thanksgiving one time. It was crazy busy! During our wait in long lines, several large families in matching T-shirts identified themselves and the fact that they were on their annual vacation. One family's shirt read, "Our Dysfunctional Family Thanksgiving Vacation." I smiled and thought, "At least they're honest!"

During the holidays our culture celebrates by gathering family members together to fellowship and eating. Although it can be a wonderful time, it can also be a very difficult for many. Family dysfunctions are brought to the surface. Past hurts and unforgiveness, among other problems that have been shoved down deep through avoidance, are now forced back into our lives by having to be together. This can be a great gift, however, because avoidance never leads to healing. Only when dysfunctions are brought to the surface can we deal with them and let God heal them. As Jeremiah 6:14 (TLB) says, "You can't heal a wound by saying it's not there!"

We all know how true this is in our biological families, however, it's just as true in our spiritual family, the Church. The Church is God's family on earth, and this global people is expressed locally in each believing congregation. In a household of repentant sinners in the process of being transformed to Christlikeness, there will inevitably be dysfunction! Sinful people sin. Hurt people hurt people. Broken people act broken. And just think, we get to gather with this dysfunctional family all year round and every week! Our church families gather to fellowship and eat regularly, if not physical food, then certainly the spiritual food of the Word and Holy Communion. So, we are given year-round opportunities to let hurts, unforgiveness, and other problems rise to the surface to be dealt with.

Like many clergy, I have a high desire to avoid conflict. I want everyone to be happy all the time. I had to learn this is a hindrance to both my and others' spiritual growth. "You can't heal a wound by saying it's not there!" When I came to know the Lord, I wholeheartedly came to believe the Bible is true. I believed Jesus physically healed because the Bible told me so. But then about a month into my conversion, I stepped on a metal pipe on the beach, cutting my foot, and needing several stitches. I thought about those scriptures, and I wanted to test my newfound beliefs. I prayed that God would take away the pain so I could walk, and immediately the pain disappeared!

The comfort from that was enormous. The Bible

was true; Jesus does heal. But the problem with this comfort soon became evident. By having no pain and walking around as I had before, the large gash on the bottom of my foot wouldn't heal. In addition to learning the lesson that I need to pray more specific prayers like, "please heal the wound," I learned that pain can be a gift from God to show us what's wrong so it can be dealt with. Pain has a purpose. This is true of emotional and relational pain as well. When there's pain in the family, it's an indicator that there's a wound that needs to be healed either in you, the other person, or more likely, both. Conflicts in our dysfunctional spiritual families are opportunities to grow in love.

One of the VITAL aspects for Church Revitalization is Authentic Community (the A in VITAL). There must be genuine love for one another expressed authentically in the Church. The first two steps to church revitalization are personal renewal with each member loving Jesus first and most, and relational renewal with each member loving one another. The church simply won't be healthy and grow if members don't really love Jesus and each other. It's about applying the Great Commandment: "'You must love the Lord your God with all your heart, all your soul, and all your mind.' This is the first and greatest commandment. A second is equally important: 'Love your neighbor as yourself'" (Matthew 22:37-39 NLT).

Authentic Community doesn't mean the absence of conflict. Genuine love for one another means learning to love sometimes unlovable family members and working through conflict in mature ways. Then, you can teach and model this way of living out community to immature believers that begin attending.

Give thanks for these opportunities to grow in love and for any dysfunction in your church family that floats to the surface. Instead of staying away from family gatherings (worship, small groups, potlucks etc.) to avoid problems, continue meeting together to allow God to show you how to love each other more fully and experience authentic community. As it says in Hebrews 10: 24-25 (NLT): "Let us think of ways to motivate one another to acts of love and good works. And let us not neglect our meeting together, as some people do, but encourage one another, especially now that the day of his return is drawing near."

CHAPTER 32:
CREATING AUTHENTIC COMMUNITY

As mentioned in the last chapter, one of the five VITAL aspects of church health is Authentic Community. Again, the principle is that there must be genuine love for one another in church if it's to be healthy and grow. Two of the most basic needs every human being has are to be loved and to belong. If you think about it, God's Kingdom experienced through the local church provides the fulfillment of both these needs.

One of the most well-known scripture verses is John 3:16 which tells us, "God so loved the world that he gave his one and only Son, that whoever believes in him shall not perish but have eternal life" (NIV). There is no greater affirmation of love than God's self-revelation in the person of Jesus Christ. The following verse in 1 John 3:16 may be less familiar: "This is how we know what love is: Jesus Christ laid down his life for us. And we ought to lay down our lives for our brothers and sisters" (NIV). These brothers and sisters are the children in God's family where we, as siblings, are called to show one another the love that God showed us in Christ. That means genuine, sacrificial love.

Church is where we put this into practice. That kind of love, when it reaches its fullness among believers, spills out into the lost world beyond the borders of the church. When Jesus prayed for the church he said, "May they experience such perfect unity that the world will know that you sent me and that you love them as much as you love me" (John 17:23 NLT). Authentic Community leads to a thriving, revitalized church and a great light to the world.

The real question is how to practically see this happen in our own churches. How can we create an environment where this kind of love for one another is fostered? The best answer I know is small groups. Sunday morning worship provides many opportunities for service to one another but doesn't provide enough interaction to create authentic community. Most of the time, worship services have loving God as their focus. The people face the front and not each other, and they concentrate on who God is and praise him for it. This is good. But the passing of the peace in liturgical churches, or coffee hours after worship are usually all that's provided on Sundays to get some connection with others. While often welcoming and comforting, these brief moments are not enough for deep connection and real love. Small groups provide an intimate setting where people can come to know one another and begin to experience true authentic community.

For me, the administration of small group ministry was one of the more challenging aspects of revitalizing the church. We tried and failed many times to get more members into small groups. Despite the challenges, they were vital to the process, and we never quit trying. Eventually, we regularly had over 50% of the church active in some mid-week small group.

Anglicans have yearly liturgical seasons based on the Christian calendar built into our common life. These different seasons provide great markers to get people into small groups. Seasonal transitions are helpful opportunities to create change in people's lives. If they're asked to join a group for a six-week season during Lent, for example, they are more likely to give it a try. If they have a positive experience, you can follow that up after Holy Week with another six weeks of groups through the season of Easter.

I learned a lot about small groups from Steve Gladen, Pastor of Small Groups at Saddleback Church, which has over 40,000 people gathered weekly in 8,000 small groups. He's the founder of SmallGroups.net and speaks on the topic of small groups and developing healthy, biblical community. He prescribes several other times of transition that are conducive to getting people into groups, and you could always try these out: significant events, painful moments, spiritual progress, and starts and stops.

Significant events in peoples' lives such as baptisms, confirmations, pre-marital counseling, etc., provide moments where individuals or couples need to stop and engage with themselves, their leaders, and others at a deeper level. We can encourage them to take this deeper dive with certain groups. Pain also motivates people to get connected. Finances, grief, single parenting, blended families, addictions, and many more issues can be a strong pull toward attending groups for extra support. Moments of spiritual progress lead many to join small groups when they are taking significant steps in their own growth. If you have a new member class, for example, make sure you talk about small groups and offer opportunities for people to join them. Starts and stops studies can also provide times when people can jump into a new group. Starting up a new curriculum can lead to the development of new small groups, particularly if the new curriculum hits a felt need in your community. I was most successful getting people into groups by using various 40-day campaigns. These moments in members' lives, while some painful and others joyful, can all lead to one thing: new spiritual growth in the presence of other individuals on a similar journey.

CHAPTER 33:
SMALL GROUPS FOR A CHANGE

In 2 Corinthians Paul writes, "Now the Lord is the Spirit, and where the Spirit of the Lord is, there is freedom. And we all, who with unveiled faces contemplate the Lord's glory, are being transformed into his image with ever-increasing glory, which comes from the Lord, who is the Spirit" (2 Corinthians 3:17-18 NIV). As has been said many times in this book, gone are the days where, if we offered decent worship services, sermons, and various programs, we could keep and grow a good church. The context for how we live out our Christianity in North America is radically different. Christendom is gone. Our present reality is that church attendance is in a steady decline and most people in North America have a secular mindset. Missionaries are now needed in our own communities and having signs that read "Now Entering the Mission Field" as you leave the church parking lot is not enough. How we do church must change because our context changed.

This reality impacts how we do community in small groups as well. The goal of small groups should not only be about loving one another better but also the making of mature, missional disciples of Jesus, Christians who "are being transformed into his image with ever-increasing glory, which comes from the Lord, who is the Spirit" (2 Corinthians 3:18b NIV). Small group Bible study for knowledge alone doesn't necessarily translate into a transformed life. Combining that knowledge with experience produces changed lives.

As you make plans for developing or strengthening small group ministry, include ways for groups to experience the faith as much as learning about it. Two small group programs I know about can be utilized to help make this happen:

1. **Rooted:** This is an excellent small group program. Grace Anglican Church in Fleming Island, FL, uses Rooted as the second part of their spiritual formation process (their T in the VITALs) as a follow up to The Alpha Course. Rooted covers the essentials of becoming a mature, missional disciple of Jesus, and encourages experiences that put them into practice. I participated in a Rooted group expecting just another small group study and was pleasantly surprised with how real it allowed participants to be and how the activities helped move information from the head to the hands through application. I saw both long-time church members and brand-new believers transformed. The group members grew in both love for each other and in missional maturity in Christ. I found

myself wishing I learned about the program earlier! To find out more about Rooted and learn how to bring it to your congregation, you can visit the website at www.experiencerooted.com.

2. **Church-wide Campaigns:** The reason campaigns work is what is referred to as "the power of alignment." For usually 40 days, or six weeks, the whole congregation is aligned to one subject. They are hearing a weekly message, studying a small group curriculum, reading daily devotionals, experiencing spiritual practices, and memorizing Scriptures all on the same topic. Many campaigns exist for purchase. You can find some at www.pastors.com and look for "campaigns," or at www.christianbook.com and look for "church-wide campaigns." They are user friendly and will come in a box for you to open and follow the instructions! After buying and doing several campaigns with our congregation, our leadership team better understood the essential components including the need to add experiences, and we started creating our own. You could do that, too!

These are just two ideas that I'm tossing out there to help jump start your small groups. What are your ideas? What have you seen that helps reach and transform lives in the love of Jesus Christ?

CHAPTER 34:
FIVE WAYS TO MORE RELATIONSHIP AND LESS RIGIDITY

I've never been caught up in trying to understand the different generations like Boomers, Gen X, or Millennials. At their core, human beings are all sinners and need Jesus. All have deep needs to be loved, to belong, and to have significance regardless of their generational trends. Early on in ministry, I got annoyed with my fellow Gen Xers who complained about and resisted "programmatic Boomer" churches and instead wanted everything to be "organic," whatever that meant. But then when I tried to implement small groups into my church using programs developed decades before me, it was very frustrating. I was rigid about sticking to the program that had worked in other places and times. These small group programs worked for a season but never seemed to remain stable.

Despite setbacks, I was committed to seeing small group ministry through. I knew how important they were for the relational and missional health of the church. In my frustration, I gradually became less rigid about how these groups should work, and I adopted a more "organic" approach that focused on relationships. I realized that certain people do respond to different experiences in different ways. In my church, it so happened that this less rigid approach was much more effective.

Maybe you've had similar frustrations with implementing programs to induce small groups. If that's the case, you can branch out to a more relational approach in these ways:

1. Have a core conviction that small groups are essential to authentic community. If you're not convinced, you won't stay committed. You must persevere through setbacks to make them a natural part of how your church lives together in community.

2. Admit what they teach in 12-Step programs: I can't, God can, so I think I'll let him! The Holy Spirit is much better at moving on people's hearts and helping them experience the joy and support that comes from belonging in a small group than we will ever be. So, pray for the Holy Spirit to guide you and the church in developing groups. He'll do it!

3. Create good environments for groups to gather. In the South, Wednesday nights are still considered church nights, so we used that time to gather in groups after a potluck dinner. When and where could you make it convenient for people to experience a regular group meeting?

4. Allow for natural on and off ramps. Using the church seasons every year is helpful in creating space for people to experiment with small group attendance. At the front end of a season (Lent, Easter, Fall, New Year, etc.), provide clear "on ramps" for people to join a group with the knowledge that there's an exit strategy. Often a couple weeks break after each season is just right. Everyone seems to enjoy a little break, and it gives people a chance to gracefully leave a group if it's not a fit for them.

5. Observe potential leaders and quickly give them leadership opportunities. Watching for people to whom you can delegate responsibility can help you loosen up your own need for control. The program model dictates the need for a co-leader who will eventually split off to form a new group, so when running things as a program, I would try to force people into that role to get that box checked. It didn't work well in my experience. Leadership develops better, however, when it emerges naturally. Letting emerging leaders take the lead in small group discussions or prayer times allows their confidence to increase and your confidence increase that sooner or later another group leader will be ready. It will happen, if you're looking for it.

PART 4 DISCUSSION QUESTIONS
AUTHENTIC COMMUNITY

1. Can you think of a time when you've had conflict with a church family member? Were you tempted to either get angry and fight them, or try to avoid and depart from the situation? Were you able to use that conflict to grow in love for a fellow believer, and if so, please describe?

2. Describe a time when you have experienced genuine love and community within a local church family. What made it special? How could you help others experience that also?

3. Have you experienced authentic community through a small group? If so, please described how it was beneficial to you.

4. In Chapter 33, Mark suggested a couple ideas to help jump start small groups in your church. What do you think about those ideas? What are your ideas that may be different?

5. What are some attempts toward getting a small group ministry developed in your church have you tried? What worked and what didn't? What could you do differently when you try to get them going again because they are so important to authentic community in a healthy church?

PART 5:

LAY MOBILIZATION FOR MINISTRY

CHAPTER 35:
HELPING MEMBERS
FIND THEIR MINISTRY

When I was a new rector, I came into the position excited for the possibility of helping people find their ministry. I soon heard old-timers expressing their fears: "I hope you're not planning on giving us another Spiritual Gift Inventory;" or "We've all taken spiritual gift inventories before and nothing ever happened." That initially sort of put a damper on my excitement.

Spiritual Gift Inventories seem to have been a popular technique in the church at one point, but thankfully, they were not a primary part of my own experience. In my previous position as associate priest, my primary job was to implement The Purpose Driven Church strategies in an Anglican context. I learned first-hand how important it was to help people discover more about themselves than just their spiritual gifts. Discovering spiritual gifts alone often causes people to wonder where in the church those gifts are needed and how to use them. Often, they don't find answers. By helping people also discover things like what they love to do, natural and learned skills, their personality traits, and life experiences, they were able to find the right ministries for them both inside and outside the church.

Rick Warren wrote, "The best-kept secret in the church is that people are dying to make a contribution with their lives. We are made for ministry! The church that understands this and makes it possible for every member to express his or her SHAPE in ministry will experience amazing vitality, health, and growth. The sleeping giant will be awakened, and it will be unstoppable." This concept of helping people discover their SHAPE proved very effective for me in mobilizing members into ministry.

The SHAPE acronym stands for Spiritual Gifts, Heart, Abilities, Personality, and Experiences.

SPIRITUAL GIFTS: When someone receives the Holy Spirit, he or she is given supernatural spiritual gifts to contribute to the church. Discovering what they are is essential to knowing where God wants someone to serve. Spiritual Gift inventory tests can be helpful for this but don't stop there.

HEART: What a person loves to do matters. Sometimes we must lay those things aside sacrificially for a season, but often God uses what we love to do in our service to him. Ministry is often difficult enough, and he uses difficulties to grow our character, but that's not the same as being miserable. God doesn't want us to be miserable serving him! For example, if someone discovered that they have the gift of teaching but for whatever reason really can't stand children, they probably shouldn't teach children's church!

ABILITIES: There are both God-given natural abilities and learned skills that people have, so not everything we receive we get "supernaturally." A common example is that there is no spiritual gift in the Bible called "Audio Visual," but many churches today very much need someone who is skilled in audio/visual work! Instead of finding any teenager to serve in technological areas just because teens should know technology, you can find someone who has a love for and is skilled at utilizing technology to create a better worship setting. They'll love it, be good at it, and all will benefit. There are many other abilities that can be used for God as well.

PERSONALITY: Someone's God-given personality also plays a key role in the ministry they should serve in. An extreme introvert probably should not be asked to be a greeter! Someone who can't stand routine probably shouldn't be a part of the weekly bulletin folding and stuffing team! Like spiritual gifts, extroverts and introverts and other personality types all fit together to make the church as a whole work well.

EXPERIENCES: Life experiences are a huge factor when it comes to helping people find the ministry God has for them. Their spiritual, educational, ministerial, and emotional history should be factored into their overall SHAPE for ministry. Our painful experiences, for example, can often point us to our most important ministries. We are often able to comfort others in the same way we were comforted if we are willing to let God work through us in those areas. As Paul wrote, "God is our merciful Father and the source of all comfort. He comforts us in all our troubles so that we can comfort others. When they are troubled, we will be able to give them the same comfort God has given us" (2 Corinthians 1:3-4 NLT).

My ministry experience in that first church helped "shape" me in utilizing this SHAPE idea to mobilize members into ministry. Whether or not you utilize this tool specifically, my encouragement to you is that whatever you do, help people discover who God made them to be in the many facets of their lives not just in what spiritual gifts he gave them. A well-rounded approach to self-discovery leads to well-rounded ministers.

It is important to have a system in place for people to discover their SHAPE and get plugged into service in the church. I found that incorporating a class on discovering your ministry into the "T" or Transformation to Christlikeness pathway you develop is very effective. Discovering your ministry is a part of becoming a mature disciple of Jesus, and the most effective approach I found was to sit down with people one on one after they came to the class on discovering their ministry to interview them and then quickly get them committed to a ministry that fit them. Yes, this took a bit of effort and time, but it worked.

CHAPTER 36:
FINDING FULFILLMENT
AND FRUITFULNESS IN MINISTRY

One of the biggest, ongoing challenges to having a healthy, revitalized church is having enough volunteers to do everything that needs to be done. Maybe that's a struggle in your congregation. It's the old 80/20 rule that is commonly talked about: 80% of the ministry gets done by just 20% of the people. Though that's probably accurate in most churches, it may feel more like 90% getting done by 10% of the church at times!

With too few people already doing too much, it's hard to do any additional work that needs to get done for church revitalization. It can feel overwhelming. You may need to pare down the work being done in order to focus on essentials, even if it's just for a season. Stop doing what isn't in line with your church's vision. Stop any work that isn't helping the church become more missional and build healthier disciples. Start having fewer meetings about meeting needs and find ways to actually meet more needs! What can you stop doing in order to focus on what will lead to church health and growth? Once you discover those better ways, how do you develop a process that consistently gets more people engaged in serving in those ways, overcoming the 80/20 problem?

The fifth VITAL aspect of Church revitalization (the "L" in VITAL) is Lay Mobilization for ministry. Healthy churches move people from unchurched and ineffective to mature members and ministers who go out on mission. Healthy churches build an army out of the attendees, contributors out of consumers! As noted in the previous chapter, whatever process or pathway you develop to move members into ministry, it's important that it allows them to discover who God made them to be. Each of us has been wonderfully made by God to serve him in some way(s).

The principle for lay mobilization is this: a person's make-up determines their ministry. Who God made someone to be determines what he wants them to do. Too often we flip that around in the church. We are reactionary. Where there is a need and someone nearby is breathing and willing to work, we stick them into service to meet the need. This does fill an immediate need, however, if what they are doing doesn't match who God made them to be, they can quickly become frustrated, burn out, and quit (and probably didn't do that good of a job in the meantime anyway!). On top of that, they can be hurt or feel like a failure and will not be willing to serve in the future.

The better option is to help people discover who God made them to be and match them to a ministry that best fits them. If there is no current ministry that fits them, maybe you could work with them to start a new one! God has each mature believer in your church for a reason.

This discernment is accomplished through some combination of heart, head, and hands learning. In the previous chapter, we discussed the SHAPE approach, determining a person's gifts, skills, and desires in a holistic way. Once people have an idea of what they'd like to do, they can continue to learn through trial and error. Let people know there's no shame in stopping a work or passing it on to others if it's not a good fit. Give them a natural "out" if needed. This will simply encourage them to continue discerning the right ministry for them.

But what about those pesky needs that keep popping up? Do you just ignore them if no one is around to meet them? Maybe, and then when it's not getting done, it may prompt someone to come forward. Sometimes there are seasons where what you want to get done can't get done. The reality is that leading a church on mission is messy. Sometimes, willing members may minister in areas that aren't a good fit for a season, and that's okay, if they know it's temporary. It's just part of being in a family.

Here's the thing, we all have both primary and secondary ministries. Primary ministries serve where God made a person to be; secondary ministries serve wherever a person is needed. Too often, we focus on the secondary ministries driven by need, and we never help people find their primary calling because they're stuck doing what must be done rather than what they want to do. Flipping that focus and making secondary work temporary with a bent on finding primary service for each mature member gives individuals fulfillment and leads to fruitfulness in your church.

PART 5 DISCUSSION QUESTIONS
LAY MOBILIZATION FOR MINISTRY

1. Have you ever been asked to serve in a ministry because there is a need and then been stuck in that ministry for too long? If so, describe how fruitful and fulfilling that was for you or not.

2. Is the more holistic approach to identifying someone's primary ministry, like using the SHAPE idea, new to you? Describe how this approach may be more effective in mobilizing lay people into ministry rather than just using spiritual gift inventory.

3. What is your church's system or plan to mobilize the laity into ministry? Can you describe it quickly and easily to someone? If someone was new to your church family and wanted to serve, would it be easy for them to figure out how to do that?

4. If your church doesn't have a system or you answered no to the second and third questions in

#3, what are some ways you can create or improve your system of lay mobilization?

SECTION 5:
ENACTING THE VISION

An intelligent person aims at wise action, but a fool starts off in many directions.
Proverbs 17:24 (GNT)

CHAPTER 37:
FIVE STRATEGIES
FOR INTRODUCING CHANGE

Much of the hard work of church revitalization is in leading the church through change. As I wrote in earlier chapters, there is no revitalization without pain because revitalization means change, change means loss, and whenever there is loss, there is pain. Since none of us like pain, it's natural to avoid making the necessary changes that will lead the church to health and growth. This is a major reason why church revitalization starts with renewal, not structural changes. Real personal love for Jesus, for one another, and for the lost is crucial, otherwise the pain of changing will be greater than the desire to grow. Unfortunately, when that happens and change is avoided, there's only continued maintenance at best and decline at worst for the congregation.

Those who engage church revitalization, as you're doing by reading this book, are willing to face the pain of change, often head on. There are ways to mitigate some of that pain, however, and you can find strategies to bring people through transition in the least painful ways possible. <u>Focus on the most important and easiest things to change first.</u>

What will make the biggest difference with the least resistance? A prominent church consultant once said that churches spend most of their time working on the wrong solutions to the wrong problems. It is better to identify what changes will make an impact and start with the ones that will cause the least amount of anxiety in the church body. This way you can gain small victories that build trust in your leadership and momentum for the mission until they're ready for larger changes and victories.

<u>Be a proponent of the new, not an opponent of the old.</u>

In Mark 2:22 (NLT), Jesus said, "No one puts new wine into old wineskins. For the wine would burst the wineskins, and the wine and the skins would both be lost. New wine calls for new wineskins." It's not wise to try and make the old wineskin hold new wine because both the new wine and the old skins are lost! No one benefits. But it's also not good to always throw out the old wineskin right away! It is better to honor the old and get people used to the idea of adding new wineskins one piece at a time. For example, you may want to turn a traditional worship service with mostly older people into a new contemporary service with lots of millennials. A better approach may be to keep the traditional service while adding a contemporary one allowing for adjustment and change that still honors the sensibilities of those who may have a harder time with it.

Respect and enlist support from "key influencers" in your church

Know who the people are in the church who are natural leaders, even if they are not clergy or on your governing board. These are the people who everyone looks to when a change is announced to see if they approve. If they do, others will often follow suit. One of the members I always talked to early on in my ministry about any change coming up was a woman named Phyllis. She was in her late 80s and was a positive and supportive member of the church and our mission. She was also the woman that all the other older ladies in the church looked to when a change was announced. If I took the time to talk with Phyllis about what was going to take place and helped her understood the change, she was almost always on board with it. After I would make a public announcement about it, all the older ladies would look over at her and see her nodding her approval. They would almost always be on board as well. Know who the Phyllis' are in your church. Respect their influence and enlist their support early on for change.

Call every change an "experiment"

If you call a new change an experiment, if it doesn't work, then you can say it was an education! Not every change you make in the church will work, and that's perfectly okay. When that happens, learn what you can from the experience and move on. Let it be the education it was meant to be. By calling the change an "experiment," you will keep your members' expectations realistic. It took many years, but we eventually developed a culture of change in our church where it was expected that changes would be continuously made in order to better fulfill the Great Commission. Some changes worked, some didn't, but everything was an education.

Enlist intercessors

As a young priest, I would hear older clergy I respected talk about having intercessory prayer teams and, often, a personal intercessor. It took time, but I was eventually able to identify and build trust with some mature prayer warriors. Once I did, they became the first people I enlisted when contemplating a potential change. It was only a small group, and I called them my "special forces" prayer team. They would hold the upcoming change in prayer and in confidence. It never ceased to amaze me how much better a change would go when it was supported by prayer. Who are the mature prayer warriors in your church who you can enlist to pray for you and the changes you need to lead?

CHAPTER 38:
CHANGE TAKES TIME

One of the "laws" of church revitalization is that change takes time. The last session of the American Anglican Council's Revive seminar focuses on effectively leading change in the church and developing the character to do so patiently. This is because we've learned that even if you have a good vision and strategy, if you can't lead your parishioners through change well, things will get bogged down with unnecessary conflict. Leading change over the long-haul requires patience, and I've found the following advice on how to do so helpful over the years.

As I wrote earlier, my first job as a priest included introducing Rick Warren's Purpose Driven Church into the local Anglican church I ministered in. As a first step, I took a team to A Purpose Driven Conference. We heard Pastor Rick tell a story about leading change that went something like this: "I know an airline pilot, and I asked him how sharply they could turn a plane. The pilot said they could make a 90-degree turn, but the problem with that is, the passengers don't like it very much! However, the pilot said, if we turn the plane at 30 degrees, we can fly in circles all day and the passengers don't even know we are turning." This concept proved true over the years when leading in times of change. Pivoting too suddenly causes fear. Fear often leads people to get angry or impatient. They may eventually leave. But if changes are introduced at a slower but steady pace, you can make them without adding unnecessary anxiety. Over the years, I referred to this so much that the term "30 degrees" became code word among our leadership to hold the course on the change without turning too fast.

Where I grew up in Florida, we had very soft sand. In fact, my high school football team would run in the sand to train for games. Our feet sank well past our ankles, and it was very hard work on our legs. Because of that, when I heard this analogy about change and sand, it stuck with me. The image is of a father who leads his young son on a walk in soft sand. The father, with his longer and stronger legs, can move at a faster pace than his son. If he walks faster than what his son can handle, the distance between them will grow farther apart. Eventually, the son might just sit down and quit! Of course, it would be better for the father to walk at a slower pace than he would like in order to not get too far ahead and allow the son to stay close and not lose hope. Eventually, when the son gets a little older and his legs develop more, they'll both be able to walk at a faster pace.

As a leader in the church, you may often have thought through the change before you even present it to others. You may have worked through any fears and problems associated with it, and by the time you introduce it to the congregation, you're ready to race ahead. If you do, and there's too much of a gap between you and everybody else, they may dig in their heels and refuse to follow. By intentionally leading at a slower pace, however, you'll bring the congregation along without causing them to be overwhelmed. Change is a long game. John Maxwell, a bestselling author and speaker on leadership once said, "He who thinks he is leading, and no one is following, is only going for a walk." If you don't lead in such a way that people will follow, it isn't really leadership. Ronald Heifetz, a leading expert on adaptive leadership, wrote that, "leadership is the art of disappointing people at a rate that they can tolerate."

As a young leader, I used to get frustrated because I thought church members should follow wherever I was leading at whatever pace, since it was obviously the right way to go! If they didn't follow, I would get angry at them and feel frustrated. This wasn't super helpful to the church or to my soul! I learned that not all resistance to change is the same. Although some stubborn people will resist change no matter what, many were willing to engage the process when I slowed down, explained things better, addressed their fears, and led them at a pace they could follow.

CHAPTER 39:
THREE TIMES CHANGE
MAY HAPPEN FAST

In the last chapter, we looked at the idea that change takes time. Patience in leading through transition is necessary for revitalizing a church and deepening trust. This principle is almost always true, but there are exceptions. When exceptions occur, it is still important to navigate them with wisdom from the Lord and good counsel from trusted leaders. It just means that the circumstances will allow you to move more quickly than is normal. The three times change may happen faster are:

When there is a new Rector/Senior Pastor

Popular wisdom passed on to new priests from previous generations is that once you're installed, it's best not to make any other changes for the first year. Instead, they say to take the time to build relationship, understand the culture, and earn the trust needed to bring about change later. Of course, building these relationships and earning trust are essential in the early years and will help you down the road to bring on greater changes, but I thoroughly disagree with the idea about not making changes in the first year.

In fact, when a church gets new leadership, it's often the perfect time to rapidly implement some strategic change. The simple reason is because the congregation is often expecting the new priest to make some changes! Every pastor is different and will do some things differently than how the last pastor did them, so of course, rapid change is expected by almost everyone in the church. It's often called the "honeymoon period" because members will give new leadership a lot of grace to make changes and get settled. This period will end, of course, and the "change takes time" principle will kick back in, but in the meantime, wisely chosen strategic changes implemented at that pivotal moment makes sense.

Most members also want to know their new pastor is competent to lead and not a dud! Making some initial, wisely chosen strategic changes during a time when changes are expected is a good way of establishing that confidence. Again, in case this wasn't already made clear, these first changes must be wisely chosen and made through prayer, conversation, the support of key influencers, and communicated well. One classic story illustrating what not to do is of a new rector who didn't like the tree outside his office window because it didn't let in enough sunlight. One day he went out and cut it down only to find it was a memorial tree planted in honor of a church matriarch. Needless to say, that change didn't go over well. His ministry was effectively over.

When I became a new rector, one of the first things I noticed was the lack of "visitor parking" signs. There was, however, a very nice "rector parking" sign in the best spot right up front. To me, this communicated that we were an internally focused church that put the comfort of the pastor ahead of its members or its guests. Since our mission is to love one another, show hospitality, and "go and make disciples" (Matt. 28: 19), I knew change needed to happen, and it didn't need to wait a year until I got to know everyone better. It was small and strategic enough of a change that would promote the vision of fulfilling the Great Commission. When I communicated my idea of replacing the rector's sign with visitor parking signs, I got immediate pushback. I was told we couldn't do that because one of the parish's "charter members" hand-made the wooden sign. It would have been easy for me to accept this situation, not wanting to cause unnecessary conflict or offend one of the last living charter members, and not make the change. Instead, I called up the man who made the sign and explained what I wanted to do and why. Not only was he supportive, but he offered to make the new visitor signs! He made them, we installed them, and I moved the rector sign to the back of the parking lot by the dumpster to visibly communicate that our mission isn't about us, and the needs of guests were greater than our own.

That small action showed the congregation that I was capable of leading in the face of resistance, that the mission of the church was my priority, and that we could move forward in a way that honored the past.

When there is a crisis

During the crisis that split the Episcopal Church, congregations that might have previously spent a year debating decisions about what color the new carpet should be were making rapid fire changes every week. They had to. Prolonged debating and tabling were no longer options. Changes were required and decisions needed to be made quickly. The debates were quick and purposeful, and change happened fast. A similar thing occurred during the more recent Coronavirus crisis. Many churches that resisted technology and alternative ways of worship or fellowship quickly adapted and were willing to change in order to continue functioning to some degree as a church family. Crises shouldn't be sought out or hoped for, but when they come, and they will, they can be used to make significant and healthy changes quickly.

When the congregation develops a culture of change

Just as in the analogy of the father and son walking in the sand shared in the last chapter, eventually those who follow become strengthened enough to keep up. The goal of every local church that wants to be missional and grow should be to have a congregation that is so committed to fulfilling the Great Commission that they adopt a "whatever it takes" attitude. This takes maturity and often prolonged seasons of training, but when it happens, regular adaptive change can become a normal part of how the church functions. Programs can come and go. If they work, they can be kept, but if they don't, they can be quickly replaced. When the church develops a culture of change, they come to see programs as serving God's greater purposes and are at peace with the need to transition into new ways of tackling new problems.

The challenge is to develop a congregation with this kind of culture. So, for the most part, change must happen slowly and carefully. It takes spiritually mature members to embrace a culture of change in a local church, people whose lives are so deeply rooted in their relationship with Christ and one another that external changes don't threaten their own security. These kinds of people are willing to "do church" selflessly for the sake of others and not primarily for themselves, and this kind of attitude has to permeate the whole church, both clergy and laity. It often takes years to arrive at this level of maturity and selflessness in Christ at a church-wide capacity. Once your church gets there, however, a lot can happen quickly, and it's a wonderful family journey that can last for decades.

CHAPTER 40:
NOT TAKING CRITICISM PERSONALLY

Those of you who have been or are married will know that when your spouse comes to you upset, the presenting issue is often not the underlying issue. For example, if they're upset because you forgot to take out the garbage again, the real issue isn't the garbage but a lack of follow-through, or a feeling of being unloved or uncared for, or disrespected. If you start fighting over the presenting issue, you'll never resolve the underlying source of conflict. This same idea applies when leading a church through change. There will always be resistance which often comes in the form of criticism. The immediate temptation is to get defensive and react, but it's best to avoid taking the criticism personally and assume that the presenting issue is not the underlying issue. Pause, pray, keep your own emotions in check, and try to figure out and address the deeper concern of the person criticizing you.

You may want to start that contemporary worship service to bring in a different group of unchurched people from your community. Even though you're making no change to the existing worship service, and you're not asking people to stop attending the service they enjoy, you'll find some complaining still. They might say, "Father So-and-So isn't being a real Anglican anymore." (And by "real Anglican" they mean the way they've always done it!) The temptation would be to take it personally and defend your Anglican credentials, but the underlying issue may not be your theological understanding but their fear of losing an identity that's important to them.

When it comes to changes that will lead to health and growth, there are three common causes of criticism that are often under the surface. This list isn't by any means exhaustive, but it's a good place to start. If you can learn to recognize these issues in people and address them, it will help you better navigate leading change.

1. **The Care Issue:** People often fear that their needs will no longer be met due to certain changes. I had people come into my office upset because to them I cared more about newcomers than I did them. In my earlier years, I might have responded with something like, "Well, kind of, because I know you'll be in Heaven when you die, but I'm not so sure about them!" That never went over well. I thought they just didn't care about lost people. I later realized that for some people that was true; however, for many, they weren't necessarily against growth or the Great Commission but were simply concerned about being cared for, too. Newcomers and old-timers all need love in their own way whether they're seasoned Christians or not. Their

deeper issue was that new people coming in would sideline them. I came to reassure existing members that I did care for them. It took some preaching, teaching, and a lot of personal conversations, but they eventually came to understand that while growing wasn't optional because of the Great Commission, there were ways I was willing to provide for their ongoing care as my parishioners. It's possible to do both.

2. **The Control Issue:** The need for control often causes problems in human relationships, and the church is no different. Change that leads to health and growth can mean that some people won't be as involved as they once were, causing them to lose a sense of control. They can resist change and become critical because they don't want to lose their influence in some area of church life. Sometimes people can be stubborn and unrepentant in this need for control, but often it reflects a desire to belong and to have purpose within the community. This is where having a compelling and clear vision for fulfilling the Great Commission is so important. Helping people see beyond their own need to control and have influence ultimately helps them towards greater love and humility. You can also reassure them that as the church grows, there will be more work to be done and greater ways their gifts and skills will fit in with what God is doing. They don't have to maintain control to know their significance to God and the Church.

3. **The Comfort Issue:** Many will be critical of you
    when you lead change because they want to avoid
    pain, since change implies loss, and loss implies
    pain. No one likes pain, and some people are not
    prepared mentally to face and deal with it. Certain
    individuals may be comfortable with how things
    are, even if the church is declining, and may be
    unwilling to move into discomfort for the greater
    good. They don't want to lose what they know and
    love, and they don't want to suffer. As Christians,
    we must be willing to enter suffering for the sake
    of others as Jesus did. His prayer at Gethsemane
    was, "Father, if you are willing, take this cup from
    me; yet not my will, but yours be done" (Luke
    22:42 NIV). He was willing to experience extreme
    discomfort for the joy set before him. God may not
    be calling us to martyrdom, but he does call us to
    self-sacrifice to whatever degree is needed for the
    sake of others. Those who struggle with this can be
    talked to, counseled, and prayed with to help them
    let go and embrace "the mind of Christ" during the
    change.

The foundation of all these sources of criticism is
selfishness, and they are rooted in spiritual immaturity. It
takes the development of humility, through patience and
perseverance, in all those who find themselves at odds with
change but who want to be different. As members learn to
work through these barriers, they become mature in their
relationship with Christ and each change becomes easier
for them. For these critical individuals, change in the

church becomes an opportunity for change in the heart. Helping them navigate this change is shepherding them to greater spiritual health.

This is a good example of why focusing on church health is better than focusing on church growth. Healthy churches have a strong "T" in the VITALs and will effectively help people mature in Christ, and a strong "A" that will provide care for all members while growing, all while proactively pursuing the "V" to go out on mission which will lead to numerical growth.

As you lead through change and transition, try to look for and help people address these deeper concerns. Engaging them and their fears takes time and effort, but it will lead to more faithful parishioners, deeper relationships, and a more peaceful experience of leading the revitalization of your church!

SECTION 5 DISCUSSION QUESTIONS
ENACTING THE VISION

1. Go back and review the five strategies for introducing change in chapter 37 in order to answer the following:

    a. What are some changes you could make in your church that will make the biggest difference with the least resistance?

    b. Is there a new ministry you could start without having to "kill" an old one?

    c. Do you know who the "key influencers" are in your church? How could you better engage them to help in the changes that need to be made?

    d. Do you know who the prayer intercessors are in your church? How could you better enlist their support in making the changes that need to be made?

2. Have you ever experienced a time when a change was made too fast in the church and it didn't

work? If so, please describe. How could moving more slowly but still moving forward be more effective?

3. In Chapter 40, Mark described three areas that often are at the core of criticisms during change. How could you address people's care needs in order to better continue leading necessary changes? How could you address people's control issues in order to better continue leading necessary changes? How could you address people's comfort issues in order to better continue leading necessary changes?

EPILOGUE:
THE COST OF REFORMATION

If you look back over the first two millennia, about every 500 years there has been some sort of significant event or reformation in the life of the Church. Around 500 AD, with the collapse of the Roman Empire, there was the rise of the monastic with Pope Gregory the Great. Around 1000 AD was the Great Schism between the eastern and western churches, and then around 1500 AD was the Reformation in the West. One of those reforms was the English Reformation, which led to the establishment of the Church of England. Now, around 2000 AD, it seems we are in a new reformation of the Church. I, among others, believe a major aspect of this reformation, when history books are written about it, will be the rise of the local church.

If you and your local church will apply the principles and ideas in this book by focusing first on renewal (especially in your love for Jesus, each other, and unsaved people), establishing a clear and actionable vision grounded in the Great Commission (by reaching a specific unchurched people group around you and making them Jesus' disciples), working diligently and in a balanced way in all five VITAL areas, and leading well through change, then your local church will be part of this historical reformation!

Remember, when it comes to the church bigger is not necessarily better; smaller is not better; but healthier is better. If your church is healthy and fulfills your local "niche" in the place you are planted, you will do your part in God's master plan of establishing his Kingdom on earth as it is in heaven. Your church doesn't have to do everything, but it is called to do the part God has for you. If you do that and let every other local church do their assignments, then even the whole Church around the world can be revived.

We know it will cost us, and the road is not easy. This revitalization, even at the local level, takes courage and determination. It's like embarking on a long road trip. The importance of asking questions before committing to the journey can't be overstated. Can you afford this trip? Are you physically able to make the journey? Will everything at home be taken care of when you're away? There is much to consider before heading off.

Church revitalization is a spiritual journey requiring just as much, if not more, consideration. As a congregation, it's important to count the cost of change and decide if your church is ready to start the process. Jesus taught, in Luke 14:28-30, on the cost of being his disciple: "Don't begin until you count the cost. For who would begin construction of a building without first calculating the cost to see if there is enough money to finish it? Otherwise, you might complete only the foundation before running out of money, and then everyone would laugh at you. They would say, 'There's the person who started that building and couldn't afford to finish it!'" (NLT)

The following are some aspects to consider in order to count the cost before committing to embarking on your local reformation:

Location

Is your church in the right place for growth? Does the makeup of the existing membership match the surrounding community? If not, can the members learn to connect with the surrounding community? Is the church's physical location highly visible and easily accessible or is it hidden and hard to find? A difficult but important question to ask is, "Does this church need to die and then be reborn?"

I've written a lot about the church I led in Jacksonville, Florida, where the neighborhood changed around the church over several decades before my arrival. The location was good, highly visible, and easily accessible, and there was a large enough unchurched population to support potential growth. Since the existing members didn't match the surrounding, unchurched population, however, a fair question for us was whether we should move to another part of town with a growing population that better matched our membership. If not, could we adapt and learn how to reach our neighbors for Christ? It was an easy decision for us. We stayed, did the hard work of adapting, and experienced revitalization right where we were. For us this made sense, but for you the answer may be different.

Leadership

Healthy and committed leadership, both clergy and lay, is essential to a church being revitalized. Some important questions for priests to ask themselves are: am I the right person to lead this change? Could I be more effective somewhere else? Is this the kind of church I should be pastoring? Do I match the congregation and the community?

Every rector is in a leadership role, but not every rector is called to lead the change required for revitalization. The American Anglican Council, in partnership with Asbury Seminary, recently created a Church Revitalizer Assessment available at www.churchrevive.org. It is a simple assessment tool that helps answer the question, "Should I try to lead a church through revitalization or not?"

All leaders aren't called to the same ministries, and that's okay. As the Apostle Paul wrote in 1 Corinthians 12: 29-30 (NLT): "Are we all apostles? Are we all prophets? Are we all teachers? Do we all have the power to do miracles? Do we all have the gift of healing? Do we all have the ability to speak in unknown languages? Do we have the ability to interpret unknown languages? Of course not!" For a pastor called to church revitalization, it is very hard work, but if someone is not called to it but tries anyway, the work becomes almost impossible.

Some questions regarding lay leadership are: do the laity have the energy and commitment to make those changes? Are the laity ready to "roll up their sleeves" and get involved in the revitalization process, or do they expect the priest to do it all since they are the "professionals"? St. Paul tells us in 1 Corinthians 12 that ministry in the church, including church revitalization, is an "all-hands-on deck" event. Lay leaders must share in the adaptive leadership process and not just expect clergy to do it all. Making sure the laity are on board is essential to knowing whether you have the resources as a congregation to move forward.

Longevity

Church revitalization takes time. There are no silver bullets or quick fixes. As we say in our Revive seminar, "We can teach you how to grow your church; we just can't teach you how to do it quickly." So the question to consider about longevity is this: are the leadership, both clergy and lay, willing to give the rest of their lives to serving this local church? If the answer is no, you probably shouldn't embark on the journey, at least not yet. Now, to be clear, lay people do move away and clergy will be called by God to serve other ministries, but the attitude while serving in your congregation should be a willingness to help fulfill the Great Commission and Great Commandment "until death do us part". They have to be all in!

Longevity also builds deep relationships and helps with trust between clergy and laity. Trust allows for taking more risks, and taking risks is necessary for revitalization. High turnover in leadership creates instability and extra resistance to change. Long-time members might think, "Why should we try that change? You're just going to leave and someone else will come in and do something else." The knowledge that you and the leaders around you are all in for the long haul will reduce this resistance and foster hope for greater stability.

Despite the challenges of facing these answers, it's important to count the cost by asking the tough questions before your journey of revitalization and reformation begins. No matter how hard things look, remember that God is for you and not against you. He is with you. There is always hope and a future with Him, so as you begin to count the cost, "be strong and courageous. Do not be frightened, and do not be dismayed, for the Lord your God is with you wherever you go" (Joshua 1:9 ESV).

For more information on the American Anglican Council, visit www.americananglican.org. If you would like to host a Revive seminar for your congregation, you can find out more information at www.churchrevive.org. Be sure to contact the Rev. Canon Mark Eldredge for additional steps for moving forward in church revitalization by emailing him at meldredge@americananglican.org.

ABOUT THE AUTHOR

The Rev. Canon Mark Eldredge was born near Buffalo, NY but escaped the frigid north for life in sunny Palm Coast, FL. Life without Christ, however, was not so sunny, and after years of wandering and wondering, he gave his life to Jesus Christ and began to pursue life in His Church. Canon Mark received his Bachelor of Science from Florida State University and his Master of Divinity from Trinity School for Ministry in Ambridge, PA.

After serving as an associate priest for three years at an Episcopal Church in Midland, TX, Canon Mark moved to Jacksonville, FL, to be the senior pastor of Epiphany Episcopal Church. While leading that church through revitalization, he also moved the congregation into what became the Anglican Church of North America (ACNA). After substantially growing and leading that church for 14 years, Canon Mark continued his vocation of bringing revitalization to churches by joining the American

Anglican Council (AAC), a non-profit ministry in partnership with the ACNA dedicated to developing, equipping, and reforming the Church in North America and around the world. Canon Mark is the Director of Anglican Revitalization Ministries for the AAC and is passionate about helping local congregations better fulfill the Great Commission in our times. He leads Revive workshops across North America and has coached pastors and lay leaders into greater opportunity for growth and mission.

Canon Mark also serves a similar role as the Canon for Congregational Health for the ACNA Gulf Atlantic Diocese based in Jacksonville, FL. He is married to his best friend, Ame Eldredge, and has three children, ages 26 to 16, and one grandson.

ACKNOWLEDGMENTS

I want to thank Canon Phil Ashey for his vision and leadership of the American Anglican Council, especially for helping to build up and defend Great Commission Anglicanism by equipping local churches in need of revitalization. And for my amazing co-workers at the American Anglican Council for without whom this book would not have been properly edited and published – thank you.

And I'd especially like to thank my wife and best friend, Ame, who lovingly supports me traveling the country, working to help revive local Anglican churches.

Made in the USA
Coppell, TX
05 January 2023